Xunzi and Early Chinese Naturalism

SUNY series in Chinese Philosophy and Culture

Roger T. Ames, editor

Xunzi and Early Chinese Naturalism

Janghee Lee

State University of New York Press

Published by
State University of New York Press, Albany

Printed in the United States of America

For information, contact State University of New York Press, Albany, NY
www.sunypress.edu

Production by Michael Haggett
Marketing by Anne M. Valentine

Library of Congress Cataloging-in-Publication Data

Lee, Janghee.
Xunzi and early Chinese naturalism : Xunzi's concept of xin and his ethical theory / Janghee Lee.
p. cm.—(SUNY series in Chinese philosophy and culture)
Includes bibliographical references and index.
ISBN 978-0-7914-6197-6 (hardcover : alk. paper)
ISBN 978-0-7914-6198-3 (pbk. :alk.paper)
1. Xunzi, 340-245 B.C.—Ethics. 2. Confucian ethics. I. Title: Xunzi's concept of xin and his ethical theory. II. Title. III. Series.

B128.H7L4 2004
171—dc22

2004015113

10 9 8 7 6 5 4 3 2 1

Contents

Chapter 1

Introduction

Xunzi 荀子[1] is less colorful than most other major, ancient Chinese philosophers. He lacks Zhuangzi's brilliant, literary imagination and falls short of Mencius's rhetorical skill in providing heart-felt illustrations. It also seems that Xunzi lacks Confucius's vibrant character. His writing style is dry and repetitive, and its tone is sometimes fairly conservative. While Xunzi can be said to be very perspicacious in making his points, he does not leave much room for interpretation. In short, Xunzi neither inspires cosmic imagination, nor touches the human heart deeply.

What, then, is the reason for the recent burgeoning interest, particularly among Western philosophical scholars, in Xunzi?[2] The fact that, notwithstanding his apparent philosophical perspicacity, the more one explores the *Xunzi,* the more enigmatic it appears, seems to invite scholarly curiosity. As clearheaded as Xunzi appears, he makes many intriguing and even seemingly contradictory statements regarding central philosophical issues. The following paragraph by David Nivison is worth citing to show how Xunzi's seemingly inconsistent arguments puzzle Western scholars:

> Xunzi argued that language, understood as names for things, is artificial, having been invented and decreed by the sage kings to satisfy human and administrative needs; yet he also thinks the language we have is right, and deplores the confusions of the sophists who treat names as merely conventional. He thought that the sage kings likewise created "rites and norms," i.e., the ordinary moral rules and standards of civilized society; and yet he also thinks that these rules and

> standards are universally binding on us and are not merely conventions. And when he tries to analyze the reasons an individual has for accepting the moral order [. . .], he tries to show that a cool calculation will lead one from one's ordinary desires to acceptance of the moral "Way" as the best means of optimizing satisfactions. Yet when he explains how one should "cultivate oneself" [. . .] so as to make this acceptance effective, he portrays the cultivated gentleman as one who loves the "Way" so that he is willing to die for it, as one who has trained himself to think, see, say, do only what is right, as one who has been transformed by this "learning" so that it penetrates his entire being. And at times Xunzi bursts out in paeans of praise of the "rites" and the "gentleman" as having a place in the cosmic order coequal with heaven and earth [. . .].[3]

In short, Xunzi sometimes looks like a genuine "conventionalist" or "nominalist" regarding language and ethical systems (rites or rituals, *li* 禮). However, he also seems to hold a "realist" position about these issues. He sometimes appears to be a flexible pragmatist, and at the same time, gives the impression of being a staunch conservative critic against all other philosophical schools, even particular Confucian camps. While he appropriates a variety of different philosophical outlooks, he always maintains a distance from them.

As Nivison's analysis implies, recent Western scholars' attempts to make sense of Xunzi's philosophy often rely on Western philosophical concepts or categories such as "realism," "nominalism," or "relativism." However, their efforts seem to pay insufficient attention to the context in which Xunzi shaped his own philosophical agenda; in other words, they seem to be too preoccupied with making sense of Xunzi's philosophy according to Western philosophical categories and forget to ask what the central philosophical problem was for Xunzi himself. In my understanding, Xunzi's overriding concern was with the "naturalistic" tendencies in the philosophy of his time. A careful examination of how Xunzi developed his notion of *xin* (heart-mind, mind-heart, heart, mind 心)[4] can offer a crucial clue to understanding Xunzi's overall philosophical structure.

Needless to say, the naturalism that Xunzi opposes is not equivalent to either pre-Socratic "naturalism," which tries to explain the world, not in terms of mythology, but in terms of natural elements such as water or fire, or the "naturalism" contemporary philosophers use when referring to the claim that every object can and should be studied by methods adopted from the natural sciences. By "naturalism," I mean an ancient Chinese philosophical orientation that seeks the source of normativity in the natural realm. In ancient China, the notion of "transcendence"—the notion of absolute deity or the conception of Platonic "Forms"—never occupied a central position in philosophical discourse. As a result, it seemed perfectly natural for philosophers to turn to the "naturalness," or "spontaneity" of nature to find the source of value or guidance for a way of life. For Xunzi, however, this posed a serious problem: if we take the natural realm as the source of values and resort to the way of nature for directing our ethical life and building culture and society, why do we need to pay respect to the Confucian cultural heritage, and how can we identify the role of human agency in establishing morality and culture? If we acknowledge the spontaneous way of nature as the source of value and moral guidance, how can we follow the way of nature without assuming there are distinctive human faculties that direct us to do so?

I argue that Xunzi's notion of *xin,* particularly as the faculty of "autonomy,"[5] is a response to the "naturalistic trend" of his time. The notion of *xin* as the faculty of self-governance is Xunzi's deliberate attempt to respond to the challenge of "naturalistic" philosophy by clearly identifying a human realm that cannot be confounded with the natural realm. Furthermore, the recognition that the Xunzian notion of morality, namely *li* (rituals, rites, manners 禮), is constructed by the autonomous faculties of *xin* can lead us to understand the reason why *li*-morality is both conventional and "objective" for Xunzi.

I explore the autonomous character of *xin* in Xunzi in the following six chapters. In chapter 2, I first examine the background against which Xunzi develops the notion of *xin* as the faculty of self-governance. Xunzi seems to regard Mencius and Zhuangzi as the two representatives of the naturalistic trend. Brief sketches of *xin* in both Menicus and Zhuangzi allow us to see the context in which Xunzi shapes his own notion of *xin.*

Chapter 3 examines the notions of *tian* (heaven, sky, nature 天) and *xing* (natural dispositions or tendencies, human nature 性) in Xunzi. These two notions can be considered the fundamental ground on which the naturalists establish their philosophical orientations. Through Xunzi's interpretation of these concepts, we can see both his response to naturalism as well as the path that leads him to the notion of the autonomy of *xin.*

In chapter 4, I first trace the evolution of *xin* from its earliest stage, as the seat of emotions, desires, and intellect, to Xunzi's autonomous, supervisory faculty. This examination shows that Xunzi's notion of the autonomy of *xin* is a concept deliberately devised to deal with the problem of the unity of *xin* in self-cultivation. By endowing *xin* with the faculty of self-governance, Xunzi renders *xin* an active agent of self-cultivation and the seat of all psychological phenomena at the same time. We notice that *xin,* as the seat of all psychological phenomena encompassing *xing*-like dispositional tendencies, includes the sense of appropriateness (*yi* 義). This is one of the most important points in Xunzi's moral psychology: the sense of appropriateness serves not only as the basis on which the autonomous *xin* deliberates and chooses a course of action on a given occasion, but also as one of the crucial reasons that the Xunzian notion of morality is not merely conventional.

I divide my discussion of the autonomous aspect of *xin* in Xunzi into both cognitive and volitional aspects. The primary function of *xin* as the faculty of self-governance can be said to be "reflective or critical" thinking to assess and guide first-order desires and emotions. This implies that *xin* is able to choose between the various sets of emotions and desires against natural tendencies or inclinations inherent in humans. Xunzi calls the resultant choice or action "deliberative exertion (*wei* 偽)." Persons, for Xunzi, can transform their natural inclinations only through the accumulation of "deliberative exertion." This "deliberative exertion" is based on knowledge gained through the combination of objective facts and subjective cognitive function. Xunzi puts equal stress on *xin*'s cognitive function of confirming empirical knowledge and on the empirical source of knowledge. What is noteworthy in Xunzi's moral epistemology is that the categorization of things that are the same and those that are different is regarded as the most basic knowledge, and is treated as being continuous with the normative evaluation of things, namely, the distinction between what is noble and what is base.

"Deliberative exertion" posits two things: first, an agent has a volitional power that allows his or her critical thinking to be unaffected or impaired by desires and emotions. Second, the exercise of volition follows *xin*'s judgment of what is reasonable. The second assumption raises the question: Can there be an occasion on which *xin*'s judgment misleads the exercise of the volition of *xin?* Xunzi replies that there are abundant occasions on which persons misjudge things, due to *xin*'s preoccupation with partial aspects of things. The remedy for this obsession or attachment is to recover *xin*'s qualities of emptiness (*xu* 虛), unity (*i* 一), and placidness (*jing* 靜), which will enable it to see things in a comprehensive, holistic way. Xunzi calls this holistic perspective *dao.*

Chapter 5 examines how *li*-morality can be deemed nonarbitrary in spite of Xunzi's acknowledgment that it was invented by the sage-kings, and how *li*-morality can be connected to the notion of the autonomy of *xin*. For this examination, I first look at Xunzi's contention in his theory of "the proper use of names (*zhengming* 正名)": names, though conventional artifacts, are not merely conventional. For Xunzi, just as measurement, which was created to satisfy the human need to measure the world, should reflect the world in order for it to work properly, names, though human conventions, should not be arbitrary or independent of the world in order for them to be good names. What Xunzi's doctrine of *li* fundamentally shares with his theory of language is that the distinction between things that are the same and those that are different and the discrimination between what is noble and what is base serve as the basis on which to build both theories. Put differently, "making distinctions (*fen*

分)" is, for Xunzi, the primary function for both language and *li*. In addition, *li* touches on the "performative" aspect of language. Naming things not only reflects the world as it is, it also serves to shape the world as it should be. The most fundamental assumption in the theory of *li* is that it can bring about an orderly society. By making social distinctions explicit and having them internalized by the members of society, *li* can make society harmonious and free of conflict. Based on these similarities, we can infer how Xunzi establishes his notion of *li* as an unconventional moral theory. The sage-kings created *li* to bring order to society. However, because *li* is inseparable from the sense of appropriateness, which is directly connected to what is reasonable, it is neither arbitrary nor unreasonable.

In the final section of chapter 5, I deal with the relationship between *li* and the autonomous *xin*. Here, I suggest several reasons that it is reasonable for the autonomous *xin* to choose *li* as the best possible solution to the problem of moral self-cultivation and the establishment of an orderly society. I first point out that *li,* though created out of the need to cope with a disorderly sociopolitical situation, is firmly grounded on *xin*'s ability to comprehend what is reasonable and appropriate. Second, I mention the connection between Xunzi's assertion that persons should transform their natural tendencies and the notion of *li* as a "practice." That is, *li* can be deemed one of the best ways to transform first-order emotions and desires into second-order emotions and desires. I also emphasize that *li,* as the concrete embodiment of *dao,* perfectly fits the Xunzian notion of "concrete rationality," which seeks a practical guide for cultivating a moral character that can adjust to changing circumstances without losing sight of the holistic picture. Finally, I offer a reconstructive narration of how a sage-king who initiates the creation of *li* can become a sage-king without the knowledge of *li*. Through this, I observe that, without the initiation of autonomous *xin, xing* can never be transformed, and that, without the deliberative capacity of *xin, li* can never be invented. Once people recognize that human psychological structure, as well as the structure of nature, is deeply reflected in *li,* they no longer see *li* as a merely conventional, suppressive custom or morality, but voluntarily adopt it as their best available moral guide for becoming virtuous and forming a flourishing society.

Chapter 6 compares Xunzi's notions of the autonomy of *xin* and *li*-morality with the Kantian notions of autonomy and morality. In this comparison, it is apparent that while Xunzi's moral philosophy can be viewed as a response to ancient Chinese naturalism, Kantian ethics can be seen as a response to the modern, mechanistic, scientific view of nature. In this respect, there are some similarities between them. Both Kant and Xunzi consider the task of their moral philosophy to be securing the ground of human morality differently from the way of nature. Both stress the importance of human agency in constructing morality. Also, both take the faculty of critical reasoning, unimpeded by emotions and desires, to be the central constituent of the notion of autonomy. However, they are fundamentally separated by their different views of nature. While Kant does not reject a materialistic, scientific view of nature, Xunzi criticizes not the organicist view of nature that he and the naturalists share, but the way the naturalists approach the relationship between humankind and nature. Accordingly, whereas Kant builds morality on a strict ontological separation between the human ethical realm and the natural phenomenal realm, Xunzi attempts to retain the continuity between human morality and the natural world, while underscoring the significance of human constructive effort in establishing morality.

Chapter 7 explores why Xunzi has, more often than not, been neglected throughout the history of Chinese philosophy. For this examination, I borrow Li Zehou's observation that all schools of Chinese thought ascribe formidable power to the subject so that the objective natural world becomes infinitely malleable to the moral will of human agency. I call this idea "subjective volitionism." On this perspective, what I call "naturalism" is just the other side of "subjective volitionism"; it is the naturalistic characterization of the moral subject as continuous with the spontaneous way of nature that offers the cosmological ground for "subjective volitionism." In contrast to naturalism, Xunzi bases the continuity of human morality and *tian* on the recognition of the difference between the way morality should be established and the spontaneous way of the natural world. This Xunzian approach to the relationship between humankind and the natural world would have been seen as less than favorable and even threatening to the volitionistic moral subject endorsed by mainstream Confucianism as the proper model for personhood.

My study of Xunzi's notion of the autonomy of *xin* and its relation to *li*-morality is neither an exegetical exercise nor a strictly philosophical assessment of the validity of Xunzi's philosophy. Rather, it might be called a "philosophical reconstruction"[6] that renders Xunzi's position philosophically plausible in its own terms. Put another way, I attempt, on the one hand, to situate Xunzi's philosophy in the proper historical context of Chinese philosophy, and on the other, to give the best philosophical interpretation of Xunzi's position. Accordingly, my study does not aspire to be the definitive interpretation of the text, the *Xunzi*, or an attempt to vindicate Xunzi's philosophy in a contemporary philosophical sense. Instead, I hope that my study turns out to be helpful to those who try to understand Xunzi's philosophy in its own right while gaining some fruitful philosophical insights from Xunzi's philosophy.

I use John Knoblock's translation of the *Xunzi*[7] for the most part, and sometimes also adopt Burton Watson's rendition.[8] However, almost all of these translations include some modifications to convey my understanding of Chinese philosophical terms. This also applies to the translations of other

Chinese texts. Following quoted passages from the *Xunzi,* I indicate the textual reference by the chapter, section, and page number of the *Concordance of Hsün Tzu* of the Harvard-Yenching Index Series[9] and the chapter and section number of Knoblock's translation. When I use Watson's translation, I add the page number from his work. The sources for all other translations from Chinese texts are provided in footnotes.

Chapter 2

Background

Introduction

Xunzi lived during the later Warring States Period (481–221 B.C.E) and probably saw the appearance of Qin Dynasty (221–207 B.C.E), the first unified Chinese empire. The Warring States Period is regarded as the most philosophically productive time in the history of Chinese philosophy. Despite the difficulties of setting up a firm chronological order, it is widely believed that all the major ancient Chinese philosophical schools, Confucianism, Daoism, Legalism, and Mohism, flourished during this period. Mencius (fourth century B.C.E) provided Confucian ethics with a firm ground by claiming that Confucian morality stems from our natural, emotional propensities. Zhuangzi (fourth century B.C.E) refined the concepts of Dao and spontaneity, attacking all the other philosophical doctrines, particularly Confucian morality, as arbitrary human conventions that prevent one from attaining authentic personhood. Mohism promoted self-sufficient, frugal, livelihood and maintains "impartial caring" based on the utilitarian idea and the concept of *tian* (heaven, sky), and later developed into a school, the Later Mohism, that focused on the analysis of language. Legalism was the last and most influential school in helping the Qin state to achieve the first unification of China. Han Fei (died 233 B.C.E), the most notable philosopher among the Legalists, promoted social engineering strictly based on law, reward, and punishment.

Mencius, Zhuangzi, and the Later Mohists all preceded Xunzi, and the two most famous Legalists, Han Fei and Li Si, were said to have studied under Xunzi. Xunzi certainly knew Mencius, Zhuangzi, the Later Mohists and the contemporary philosophical doctrines and has been thought to pave a way to the development of Legalism.[1] Xunzi is most famous for his doctrine that human *xing* (nature, natural propensities) is bad and for his emphasis on the notion of *li* (ritual, rite, etiquette, manner). Xunzi's doctrine of human *xing* is a direct response to Mencius's claim that human *xing* is good. Mencius persuades kings and state lords to accept that they are born with sympathetic hearts that cannot bear to see the suffering of others. They are originally good, but they just do not exert their potential to be good. If they govern their people with good hearts, all the rest will be resolved and, ultimately, they will rule over the world under the heaven. Disagreeing with this Mencian concept, Xunzi claimed that, since people are born with the need to satisfy their insatiable desires, it is very dangerous to let the people trust their natural instincts. Without hard work and the study of Confucian cultural heritage, particularly *li,* which would enable persons to control and transform the instinctive impulses of their desires and emotions, there would be no hope for them to become decent human beings and construct an orderly and flourishing society. Xunzi's appeal to *li* and his doctrine of *xing* target Mencius as well as other philosophical rivals, most notably Zhuangzi. Zhuangzi's philosophy is based on his belief that all the artificially formed artifacts—personal habit, convention, and culture—are against the nature of *dao* characterized as "spontaneity," such that they prevent people from gaining authentic personhood. For Xunzi, Zhuangzian Daoism is simply the result of ignorance of the fundamental distinction between nature and human beings. While nature can be characterized in terms of spontaneity and effortlessness, humans remain humans only if they make "deliberative efforts" to produce and sustain morality and culture.

This general information about Xunzi's philosophy does not exhaust scholarly studies on him. One of the main reasons scholars continue to produce articles about him is that Xunzi's philosophy in its entirety, despite its clarity in presenting each claim, seems to be inconsistent: if human *xing* is bad, how can the transformability of personhood be argued? If *li* is just human convention, how can it claim the authority to demand people to absorb it thoroughly? We will find an important hint in answering to these questions by turning our attention to Xunzi's often neglected notion, *xin* (heart, mind, heart-mind, mind-heart 心).

The notion of *xin* is one of the most important concepts in the history of Chinese philosophy. Generally speaking, while much of Western philosophy can be said to hinge on the notion of a rational agent who can investigate the world and humankind objectively, Chinese philosophy requires an agent who is able to carry out the self-transformative cultivation through which a human being can attain ideal personhood. Considering the overriding concern for self-cultivation in the major philosophical trends of Confucianism, Buddhism, and

Daoism, it is not difficult to see the importance of the notion of *xin* for these religious and philosophical schools. For example, neo-Confucianism's quarrel with Buddhism can be understood largely as the battle over how to define the nature and role of *xin*. Although there is a great difference between Buddhism and neo-Confucianism in their understanding of the world and of the nature of successful living, they both give great weight to the notion of *xin* as an agent for self-cultivation. In Buddhism, human mind, or *xin*, is, on the one hand, the source of all cravings, and thus of all illusions, and on the other hand, it is conceived as the agent that can emancipate the self from all kinds of intentional thoughts and emotions (attachments) so that the self is able to attain Nirvana. It is, therefore, natural that one of the most famous slogans in Chinese Buddhism is "making mind empty," or "empty mind (*kongxin* 空心)." For neo-Confucians who try to rejuvenate the philosophy of ancient Confucianism, this Buddhist understanding of *xin* seriously undermines the ethical dimension of the notion of *xin*. *Xin* cannot be merely empty;[2] it is the source of morality as well as the faculty that directs one's moral cultivation. Thus, it is not difficult to see that articulating and defending their notion of *xin* is a primary task for neo-Confucians in responding to the challenge of Buddhism. Because Confucians generally regard *xin* as the central faculty that directs the self to strive to attain Confucian ethical ideals, and they emphasize self-cultivation as the indispensable basis for building a flourishing Confucian society, it may not be an exaggeration to say that Confucianism hinges on the notion of *xin* more than any other school.

Despite the significance of the notion of *xin*, if one takes a look at the current literature concerning early Confucianism, one can see that it has not been given due attention. It seems that the controversy concerning the notion of *xing* (natural tendencies, incipient disposition, human nature 性) has overshadowed the attention given to the notion of *xin*. Considering that early Confucianism, particularly the *Mencius* and *Xunzi*, plays a paradigmatic role in the later development of the idea of a Confucian moral self, it seems worth exploring *xin* in early Confucianism. I believe that a close examination of Xunzi's notion of *xin* provides an excellent guide for understanding his overall philosophy. Commentators have been struggling to interpret Xunzi's seemingly inconsistent remarks about the conventionality of human morality and its "objectivity" based on a natural order or pattern. I argue that the key concept in Xunzi's philosophy is his notion of the "autonomy" of *xin*. It is here that Xunzi establishes the distinctive human realm on one hand, and retains the traditional, correlative worldview in which the realm of humankind is harmoniously connected to the natural world on the other. It will also be shown that the Xunzian notion of human agent, who possesses the autonomous *xin*, is not like Kant's autonomous agent who legislates morality based on purely abstract, universalizable principles. A moral agent in Xunzi is someone who can formulate human culture and norms by reflecting on concrete, historical experiences as well as natural order.

The following passages provide a glimpse into the Xunzian notion of the autonomy of *xin:*

> The *xin* that dwells within the central cavity is used to control the five faculties—it is called the lord provided by *tian* [heaven, nature]. (62/17/12, Knoblock 17.3a)
>
> X*in* is the lord of the body and master of the spiritual intelligence. It issues commands but does not receive commands. On its own authority it forbids or orders, renounces or selects, initiates or stops. . . . If *xin* thinks something right, it will accept it; but if it thinks something wrong, then it will reject it. (80/21/44–46, Knoblock 21.6a)
>
> The emotions being so paired, the *xin*'s choosing between them is called thinking. The *xin*'s thinking something and the natural abilities' acting on it is called "deliberative exertion [偽 *wei*]." (83/22/3, Knoblock 22.1b)

From the above passages, several characteristics of Xunzi's notion of *xin* can be inferred. First, *xin* is not an abstract faculty separable from bodily organs. Second, *xin* is the only faculty that actively judges and commands and does not just respond passively to external things and stimuli. Third, *xin* has the ability to choose a course of action deliberately. Although these characteristics do not offer the whole picture of *xin* in Xunzi's philosophy, they illuminate some distinctive features of Xunzian philosophy. First, it is a response to the "naturalistic" tendencies of philosophers contemporary to Xunzi, particularly Mencius and Zhuangzi. Xunzi seems to interpret the Mencian doctrine to imply that persons can cultivate their morality just by passively following *tian*-endowed, spontaneous, moral emotions. Xunzi also sees Zhuangzi's emphasis on the "spontaneity of nature" as the ultimate guide for human life as the outcome of Zhuangzi's ignorance of the distinction between the natural realm and the human realm. From Xunzi's perspective, both Mencius and Zhuangzi conflate what a person should do with what *tian* does. However, it is important to be careful here; what Xunzi emphasizes is not the "ontological" separation of humans and the world. Xunzi does not oppose a traditional, correlative cosmology in which persons can form a trinity with heaven and earth (*tiandi* 天地). In fact, he specifically affirms it: "Heaven and earth give birth to the exemplary person (*junzi* 君子), and the exemplary person puts in order heaven and earth. The exemplary person is the triadic partner of heaven and earth, the summation of the myriad things, and the father and mother of the people" (28/9/65–66, Knoblock 9.15).

The establishment of the proper realm of humankind is, for Xunzi, the most urgent and important philosophical task; what people have to do should not be confused with the mystical or spontaneous job of *tian*. What makes humans human is neither the moral emotions endowed by *tian* nor the unreflective imitation of the way of nature; it is the intellectual and volitional effort of the autonomous faculty of *xin*, which enables them to pursue creative, yet nonarbitrary, morality and build a sound and humane society.

To correctly understand Xunzi's philosophical project, particularly his notion of *xin*, it is necessary to examine the philosophical rivals against which he develops his own problematic. As has just been noted, Xunzi seems to regard both Mencius and Zhuangzi as representatives of "naturalism": Mencius is the spokesperson of the "naturalistic tendency" within the Confucian school, and Zhuangzi is the ultimate "naturalist" within Daoism. Their respective notions of *xin* seem particularly to have played a crucial role in shaping Xunzi's own conception of *xin*. We will not attempt to scrutinize the characteristics of their philosophical psychologies. Rather, our focus will be on the aspects of their notions of *xin* that Xunzi appropriates and criticizes.[3]

Xin 心 in the *Mencius*

One of the most controversial issues in discussing the notion of *xin* in the *Mencius* is the extent to which Mencius distinguished between the meaning of *xing* (human nature, natural propensities, characteristic tendencies)[4] and *xin*. When Mencius urges rulers to examine their hearts and have "the sensitive *xin* to the suffering of others 不忍人之心" or "the *xin* of compassion or the commiserating *xin* 惻隱之心,"[5] he seems to regard *xin* as the incipient moral emotions on which one can develop one's moral character. This "sensitive *xin*" is a natural propensity of human beings and a distinctive human property, without which "man is scarcely different from beasts."[6] Mencius seems to emphasize here that morality is as "natural" to humans as are their appetites for food and sex. Hence, when Gaozi questions Mencius' claim that human *xing* is good, Mencius replies in terms of *xin* without even mentioning *xing*:

> As far as emotional dispositions (*qing* 情) go, a man is capable of becoming good. That is what I mean by good. As for his becoming bad, that is not the fault of his native endowment 才. The *xin* of compassion is possessed by all men alike; likewise the *xin* of shame, the heart of respect, and the *xin* of right and wrong. The *xin* of compassion pertains to benevolence, the *xin* of shame to dutifulness, the *xin* of respect to the observance of the rites, and the *xin* of right and wrong to wisdom. Benevolence, dutifulness, observance of the rites,

> and wisdom are not welded on to me from the outside; they are in me originally.[7]

As one more piece of evidence for an apparent identification of *xing* with *xin* we can adduce the famous "Ox Mountain" passage, in which Mencius directly relates the discussion of the *xing* of a mountain to man's moral *xin* 仁義之心.[8] It is, thus, no wonder that many traditional and contemporary commentators do not examine the Mencian notion of *xin* separately from that of *xing*.

However, there are other passages in which Mencius clearly distinguishes *xing* from *xin:* "That which a gentleman follows as his *xing*, that is to say, benevolence, rightness, the rites and wisdom, is rooted in his *xin*."[9] Here, *xin* refers to the bodily location in which moral emotions, namely *xing*, reside. In the following passage, Mencius explicitly assigns to the notion of *xin* the features that clearly distinguish it from the notion of *xing:*

> The organs of hearing and sight are unable to think and can be misled by external things. When one thing acts on another, all it does is to attract it. The organ of heart can think. But it will find the answer only if it does think; otherwise, it will not find the answer. This is what *tian* (heaven) has given me. If one makes one's stand on what is of greater importance in the first instance, what is of a smaller importance cannot displace it. In this way, one cannot but be a great man.[10]

Mencius emphasizes the function of *xin* to think and choose the moral priority in contrast to the other physical organs, which can be misled by external things because of their passivity.

If Mencian moral theory is based on "the Perfectibility Model,"[11] it can be assumed that its logical consequence is to require some kind of agency that can direct and supervise incipient, moral inclinations. In this regard, we may take the above passage to indicate that Mencius identifies *xin* as the separable moral agent from dispositional *xing*. This perplexing aspect of the notion of *xin* in the *Mencius* leads Benjamin Schwartz to view the Mencian notion of *xin* as having "two levels": in the spontaneous level, *xin* is "the natural heart of goodness," and in the reflective level, it is "the heart as the intentional organ of willing and thinking."[12] In other words, in his moral psychology, Mencius sometimes seems to use *xin* to refer to something almost indistinguishable from *xing*, and at other times, emphasizes the distinctive nature of *xin*, separable from that of *xing*. Even without examining the plausibility of Schwartz's two-level theory, we can say that the Mencian notion of *xin* is open to diverse interpretations.

My aim is not to give a full and coherent account of the Mencian notion of *xin*, but to suggest some aspects of it that prompt Xunzi to criticize Mencius and shape his own conception. It therefore suffices to say that frequent references in the *Mencius* to *xin* as a moral, emotional faculty provide enough evidence for Xunzi to conclude that Mencius neither distinguished between natural dispositions and deliberative activity, nor saw the significance of the role of *xin* in establishing morality.

XIN 心 IN THE *ZHUANGZI*

Zhuangzi represents Daoist "naturalism" in the late Warring States period. "Naturalism" denotes a unique Chinese worldview; it is based neither on a mechanical, impersonal notion of nature, nor on a shamanistic "animated" one. "Nature" or "*tian*" is what produces all the myriad things, including human beings; it provides human beings with the model or norm to follow, as well as being the source of morality. The unity of human beings and *tian* (heaven, nature, sky) is regarded as the highest achievement, which only the sage can attain. In this mode of thought the most significant issue lies in the way one understands *tian* or nature. Zhuangzi is a very radical "naturalist" in his rejection of any deliberate human activity as "falsity or fake (*wei* 偽)."[13] According to him, human customs and normative thinking or judgment, particularly Confucian values that encourage us to make a distinction between right and wrong and between noble and base, are against nature's spontaneous and undifferentiated way (*dao* 道). In this regard, it may be easy to assume that Zhuangzi is one of the main opponents of Xunzi. However, in the chapter titled "Dispelling Blindness (*jiebi* 解蔽)," Xunzi employs notions of emptiness (*xu* 虛), placidity (*jing* 靜), and unity (*yi* 一) that he explicitly borrows from Zhuangzi. This intriguing fact prompts Lee Yearley to argue that the real, "esoteric" Xunzi is much closer to Zhuangzi than we initially might think.[14] Bearing this in mind, let us take a close look at the context in which Zhuangzi refers to *xin* as empty, placid, and unitary.

First of all, it has to be pointed out that when Zhuangzi discusses *xin* as being empty, placid, and unitary, he is describing the achieved state of *xin* that can be reached only by the sage or the consummate person (*zhiren* 至人). Since the single character, *xin*, can refer to just an ordinary mind that is accustomed to making judgments, Zhuangzi seems to avoid using it when emphasizing the achieved state of *xin*. Instead, he employs various expressions: the achieved state of *xin* is described as unitary (*yi* 一) *xin*, constant (*chang* 常) *xin*, or the sage's *xin*;[15] without *xin* at all, the achieved state is expressed in mystical, esoteric terms such as the empty room (*xushi* 虛室) and the spirit tower (*lingtai* 靈臺).[16]

What, then, is the state of *xin* as empty, placid, and unitary? Regarding the conception of emptiness, we can refer to the dialogue between Confucius and Yan Hui about the meaning of "the fasting of *xin* (*xinzhai* 心齋)":

> [Confucius says,] "Make your purposes one (若一志 *ruoyizhi*)! Don't listen with the ears, listen with *xin*. No, don't listen with *xin*, but listen with *qi* (vital energy 氣). Listening stops with the ears, *xin* stops with recognition 符, but *qi* is empty and waits on all things. The way (*dao*) gathers in emptiness alone. Emptiness (*xu* 虛) is the fasting of the *xin*.[17]

The fasting of *xin* allows empty *qi* to fill up *xin*. The emphasis is on the nature of *qi* as something devoid of any sensory quality or cognitive function. This emptiness seems to refer to the unagitated state of *xin* in which it can be free of all desires and judgmental thinking. The empty *xin* is directly connected to "the oneness" of *xin*. As the above passage shows, the first step in emptying *xin* is "to make one's purpose one." To make one's *xin*, or purpose, one is not just to have one's mind concentrate on something in an ordinary sense. As carpenter Chui's fingers share in the transformation of things in drawing an exact, "true figure," the unitary *xin* is beyond the distinction between subject and object:

> When carpenter Chui drew a figure it was true to a compass or an L-square; his fingers changed along with things and did not depend on the thinking of the heart to verify. Consequently his Magic Watchtower (*lingtai* 靈臺) was a unity and he could go up and down it unobstructed.[18]

As another achieved state of *xin*, the placidity of *xin* focuses on *xin*'s ability to be undisturbed by external things and still reflect things without distortion:

> The sage is placid not because he takes placidity to be good and therefore is placid. The ten thousand things are insufficient to distract his *xin*—that is the reason he is placid. Water that is placid gives back a clear image of beard and eyebrows; reposing in the water level, it offers a measure to the great carpenter. And if water in placidity possesses such clarity, how much more must pure spirit (精神 *jingshen*). The sage's *xin* in placidity is the mirror of heaven and earth, the glass of the ten thousand things.[19]

In sum, Zhuangzi's description of the achieved state of *xin* as "empty, unitary, and placid" reflects his naturalist perspective, which emphasizes the assimilation of the human agent into the undifferentiating, spontaneous way of nature. For this purpose, the Zhuangzian *xin* has to be open to the external world without any attachment, while not being disturbed or agitated by external things. Xunzi criticizes Zhuangzi's naturalism in a succinct passage: "Zhuang Zhou was blinded by *tian* and was insensible to human beings" (Knoblock 21.4). Although a determination of the extent to which Xunzi appropriates Zhuangzi's notion of *xin* is delayed until we deal directly with Xunzi's notion of *xin*, we can, given the emphasis Xunzi puts on autonomous human activity, safely assume that Xunzi would not adopt Zhuangzi's notion of *xin* as empty, unitary, and placid without any modifications.

Chapter 3

The Notions of *Tian* 天 and *Xing* 性 in Xunzi

Introduction

Whether or not he understood Mencius and Zhuangzi correctly, it would still be a formidable challenge for Xunzi to establish his own philosophy against them. Mencian "naturalistic" ethics can, at least, be seen as a cogent solution for the problem of the source of morality, because it does not need to seek morality outside of human natural emotions and still retains its connection with *tian* (heaven, nature). The Zhuangzian natural philosophy suggests a "universal" way of life for humans, which is based on the spontaneity of nature (*ziran* 自然), and thus, can be beyond the arbitrariness of human convention. Therefore, Mencius and Zhuangzi can be said to avoid the problem of "arbitrariness" by relying on the notions of *tian* and spontaneity, respectively. Why, then, did Xunzi try to separate himself from the Mencian and Zhuangzian naturalistic trend? As has been suggested, it is because Xunzi deems that their philosophies fail to establish the "autonomous" human realm; they do not recognize the importance of the distinction between *what is just given* and *what should be achieved*. Human morality and orderly society cannot be given by just following the *tian*-endowed emotions or the spontaneous way of nature. They should be actively pursued and achieved through conscious effort. Xunzi's solution to "arbitrariness," on the other hand, is to rely on the notions of way (*dao* 道), reasonableness (*li* 理), and categories (*lei* 類), rather than the notion of *tian*. It is Xunzi's notion of *xin* that plays a crucial role in establishing his philosophy and that keeps intact the possibility of autonomous human effort, while at the same time basing it on an objective ground.

It is necessary to make a detour in examining the notion of *xin*. Chinese philosophical concepts usually defy an easy approach for analytically minded researchers. Chinese philosophers do not form a philosophical system by accumulating detailed analyses of philosophical terms. Rather, they draw a whole picture in which certain key concepts are highlighted naturally in terms of their relation to one another within this picture. Xunzi is no exception in this regard; although he is very careful in defining certain philosophical terms and drawing distinctions among them, it is not possible to fully understand his notion of *xin* without closely examining other related concepts. Hence, I first deal with the character of the notion of *tian* as the source of *xin*. Next, I will examine the notion of *xing*, which represents Xunzi's understanding of the *tian*-endowed, passive human faculties.

Tian as the Source

Characterizing the role of *xin* as the director[1] of the five faculties, Xunzi dubs *xin* "the *tian* lord (*jun* 君)" (62/17/12, Knoblock 17.3a). What does Xunzi have in mind in using the term "*tian*"? Fung Yu-lan's classification of *tian* into five different meanings can offer a good starting point for the discussion of *tian* in the *Xunzi*:

> As for Heaven or *T'ien* [*tian*], this word occurs in Chinese writings with five different meanings:
>
> 1) A material or physical *T'ien* [*tian*] or sky, that is, the *T'ien* [*tian*] often spoken of in apposition to earth, as in the common phrase which refers to the physical universe as 'Heaven and Earth' (*T'ien Ti* [*tiandi*] 天地).
> 2) A ruling or presiding *T'ien* [*tian*], that is, one such as is meant in the phrase, 'Imperial Heaven Supreme Emperor' (*Huang T'ien ShangTi* [*Huangtian shangdi*] 皇天上帝), in which anthropomorphic *T'ien* [*tian*] and *Ti* [*di*] are signified.
> 3) A fatalistic *T'ien* [*tian*] equivalent to the concept of Fate (*ming* 命), a term applied to all those events in human life over which man himself has no control. This is the *T'ien* [*tian*] Mencius refers to when he says: "As to the accomplishment of a great deed, that is with *T'ien* [*tian*]" (*Mencius,* 1b.14).
> 4) A naturalistic *T'ien* [*tian*], that is, one equivalent to the English word Nature. This is the sort of *T'ien* [*tian*]' described in the 'Discussion on *T'ien* [*Tian*], in the *Xunzi* (ch. 17).
> 5) An ethical *T'ien* [*tian*], that is, one having a moral principle and which is the highest primordial principle of the universe.[2]

> This is the sort of *T'ian* [*tian*] which the *Chung Yung* [*Zhongyong*] (Doctrine of the Mean) refers to in its opening sentence when it says: "What T'ien [*tian*] confers (on man) is called his nature."[3]

Fung Yu-lan states explicitly that for Xunzi, *tian* is "one equivalent to the English word Nature." However, recent scholars, particularly Robert Eno and Edward J. Machle, reject this interpretation.[4] Machle stresses the inadequacy of "nature" as the translation of *tian*. His point is that, although Xunzi's notion of *tian* lacks the transcendental element, it still carries the religious, spiritual dimension characteristic of the ancient Chinese worldview. Robert Eno also avoids the term, *nature,* in rendering *tian,* although his rationale is quite different. To him, the notion of *tian* is not central to early Confucians at all. It is the means by which the early "Ru" school survived the politically turbulent period, keeping their religious practice, namely "*li* 禮 (ritual)," intact. He draws this conclusion from his observation that Confucius, Mencius, and Xunzi employ the notion of *tian* in an inconsistent manner. In Xunzi's case, according to Eno, we "encounter three theories of *T'ien* [*tian*]": the first is "the theory of *T'ien* [*tian*] as non-purposive, non-normative Nature," the second portrays "this natural *T'ien* [*tian*] as normative," and the third uses *tian* "as a normative term without any direct reference to Nature at all."[5]

Both of these scholars seem to miss important points while exaggerating some aspects of Xunzi's notion of *tian*. The *tian* for Xunzi is, of course, not "nature" in the sense of a modern scientific worldview. It surely contains a religious element. As Graham aptly points out, while Xunzi's view on *tian* sometimes "looks like a 'scientific' approach to nature," "there is also in Hsun-tzu [Xunzi] a certain residual awe of the sacred in nature."[6] However, it seems that for Xunzi, the more important aspect in the notion of *tian* is not its religious character, it is its impersonal, nonpurposive character. For this allows humans a realm of autonomy. Eno's characterization of the notion of *tian* in early Confucianism also overstates the sociopolitical contexts and readily gives up an effort to understand the notion of *tian* in a coherent way. The meaning of *tian* in the *Xunzi* can be seen as having several dimensions. However, it does not have to lead us to conclude that Xunzi intentionally appropriates the notion of *tian* in an inconsistent way for the sake of preserving esoteric ritual practice. Rather, given Xunzi's overriding concern with naturalism in his time, it would be more plausible to see it as an attempt to identify the realm of *tian* more clearly according to specific contexts: whether it is in the context of defining *tian* as the origin of all myriad things, including human faculties, as well as the ultimate "aspirational end" of human effort, or in the context of distinguishing the realm of human beings from that of *tian* in a normative sense, indicating that humans ought not to follow or emulate *tian*'s way.

The controversy can be reduced to two questions. First, to what extent can Xunzi's notion of *tian* be called "nature"? Second, did Xunzi employ the notion of *tian* in an inconsistent manner? Insofar as *tian* is the cosmological source for all the myriad things and its nature is nonpurposive, the conception of *tian* resembles modern, impersonal "nature" to a significant degree. However, if we construe "nature" as something that is "mechanical, value-free, and exploitable,"[7] it seems inappropriate to render Xunzi's *tian* as "nature." Xunzi contends that the highest level mankind can reach is not outside the realm of *tian*, it is continuous with it. Is this evidence for Xunzi's intentional inconsistency, as Eno claims? Consider Xunzi's words:

> The way *tian* moves is constant: it did no special act toward Yao's survival, nor toward Jie's fall. Respond to it with good government (*zhi* 治), and good fortune will result; respond to it with disorder, and misfortune will result. Strengthen the root and regulate the expenditures, and *tian* cannot impoverish. If your nourishment is complete and your movements accord with the season, then *tian* cannot afflict you with illness. (62/17/1–2, Knoblock 17.1)[8]

This is a famous passage in the chapter, "Discourse on *Tian* (*tianlun* 天論)," quoted as evidence that Xunzi's notion of *tian* has a "nonpurposive" aspect. *Tian*'s constancy implies its own working manner independent of human intentions or wishes. It has nothing to do with the society's or with peoples' good fortune or misfortune. Later in the same chapter, Xunzi states that "flood and drought cannot cause famine, cold and heat cannot cause sickness, and strange and uncanny events cannot cause misfortune." Considering the parallel expression, we can assume that flood and drought, cold and heat, and strange and uncanny events are treated as phenomena belonging to the realm of *tian*. In this respect, *tian* is an objective natural phenomenon or condition; accordingly, it neither favors nor disfavors human life.

As several commentators have suggested, this nonpurposive *tian* is not Xunzi's invention.[9] As Graham puts it, "recognition that spontaneous process takes a course independent of man's morality had become so much the dominant trend in the 3rd century B.C."[10] It is particularly Daoist naturalists who try to strip the notion of *tian* of any anthropocentric ethical connotations. However, the underlying intention to emphasize the nonpurposive aspect of *tian* in the *Xunzi* seems to be quite different from that of Daoist naturalism. As has been observed in the discussion of *xin* in the *Zhuangzi*, Zhuangzi's philosophical direction is to return to the undifferentiated, spontaneous, natural way. In other words, while Zhuangzi's *tian*, or nature, does not conform to human conventional morality, it still suggests the norm or model for human beings to follow. In contrast, Xunzi does not seem to endorse the way of *tian* as the model for human beings:

> Although the seasons are received just the same as in an orderly age, the catastrophes and calamities will be of a different order [of magnitude] from those of an orderly age; yet you can have no cause to curse *tian*, for these things are the consequences of the way that you have followed. Accordingly, if you understand the division between *tian* and humankind, then you can properly be called "a consummate person (*zhiren* 至人)."[11] (62/17/6, Knoblock 17.1)

For Xunzi, *tian* is not only nonpurposive, it also gives no specific guide for what persons ought to do. *Tian* itself is not responsible for disaster and devastation. It is the responsibility of human beings to prepare themselves for exigent circumstances. The "consummate person" is someone who knows this and carries out the task that belongs to him.

Tian, however, does not lack a mystical dimension:

> Not to act, yet bring to completion (*buweiercheng* 不為而成); not to seek, yet to obtain—this indeed may be described as the work of *tian* (*tianzhi* 天職). (62/17/6, Knoblock 17.2a)

> Each of myriad things must be in a harmonious relation with *tian* in order to grow, and each must obtain from *tian* the proper nurture in order to become complete. We do not perceive the process, but we receive the result—this indeed is why we call it "marvelous (*shen* 神)." All realize that *tian* has brought completion, but none realizes its formlessness—this indeed is why we call it "*tian*." (62/17/9–10, 17.2b)

Xunzi does not deny that *tian*'s work is awe-inspiring. It does its work with ultimate spontaneity and brings it to completion effortlessly. Right after this passage, Xunzi claims that "only the sage acts (*wei* 為) not seeking to know *tian*."

It now seems evident that *tian,* for Xunzi, is not a mechanically governed, exploitable nature; it is a spontaneous, nonintervening nature whose magical working manner is totally different from the arduous, voluntary manner of humans. Thus, the sage or the consummate person who knows the division between *tian* and mankind not only does not seek to know *tian,* he also does "not compete with *tian* in its work" (62/17/7, Knoblock 17.2a). This is further criticism against Zhuangzi's idea of the consummate person who aspires to be "a companion of *tian*" and Mencius' claim that "for a man to give full realization to his *xin* is for him to understand his own *xing,* and a man who knows his own *xing* will know *tian*."[12] Mankind can achieve a triad with heaven and earth (*tiandi* 天地)[13] only as a result of doing his own distinctive job, namely bringing order to society: "*Tian* has its seasons; earth its resources; and man his government (*zhi* 治). This is what is meant by 'being able to form a triad'" (62/17/7–8, Knoblock 17.2a).

The characteristics of *tian* can be recapitulated as follows: the nonpurposive, nonintervening feature of *tian* is revealed in its spontaneous, magical way of working independently from human beings' strenuous and deliberate way of doing. However, the realm of *tian* is not totally inaccessible to human beings because they can participate in the order of *tian* by building a flourishing, orderly society. These features of *tian* are not likely to be seen as incompatible by Xunzi. What Xunzi tries to make clear about the notion of *tian* is not the rigid distinction between value and fact or between nature and culture. Rather, his main concern is to clarify *tian*'s role and function so that human beings do not confound their job with that of *tian*. To relate to *tian* harmoniously is not to emulate *tian*'s way, as Daoists do, it is to exercise one's own moral capability.

Nonetheless, the dualistic features of *tian,* which, on the one hand, has its own distinct way of working, and, on the other, leaves room for the participation of human beings, can still be viewed as puzzling. How can the human realm be continuous with the realm of *tian* if human beings' style of working is totally different from that of *tian?* The notion of *xin* hints at an answer to this puzzle. As we have already seen, Xunzi calls *xin* "*tian* lord." *Xin* is given by *tian*. However, it is also characteristically a faculty of self-governance. Therefore, its name is "*tian* lord." Put differently, *xin* is both a *tian*-endowed faculty in terms of its original character and a faculty of self-governance in terms of its manifest nature. It is, thus, an agent that, though firmly rooted in *tian,* is able to exercise its faculties in its own distinctive way.

In contrast to this double-dimensional *xin,* human characteristics such as sense perceptions, emotions, and desires are purely given by *tian* and act only in response to *xin*'s command or external stimuli. The generic term for these passively responsive characteristics, which have no potential for self-governance, is called "*xing*" by Xunzi. The contrast between autonomous *xin* and passively responsive *xing,* though all are given by *tian,* is the key underlying structure in Xunzi's attempt to build a moral philosophy against the naturalistic philosophical trend of his time.

Xing as Given Qualities

The Definition of *Xing*

Xunzi's most famous and controversial doctrine is that human *xing* is "bad" (*e* 惡). Given that *xing* is characterized as something given by *tian* (23.1c), does Xunzi imply that human ugliness or badness stems from *tian?* If Xunzi's *xing* is rendered as "inborn nature," how can humans be moral? What is the relationship between *xing* and *xin?* In order to answer these questions, we first need to look at Xunzi's definition of *xing*. Xunzi gives several expositions about the notion of *xing:*

> What characterizes a man from birth (*sheng*) is called his *xing* (*sheng zhi suo yi ran zhe wei zhi xing* 生之所以然者謂之性). What is produced out of the harmony of *xing,* out of the sensibilities or the organ tallying as the senses respond to stimuli, and what from birth is effortless and spontaneous are called *xing* (性之和所生，精合感應，不事而自然謂之性). (83/22/2–3, Knoblock 22.1b)[14]

First, Xunzi defines *xing* in terms of *sheng* (life, growth, to give birth to). As Kwong-loi Shun points out, scholars seem to agree that the word *xing* originated from the word *sheng,* although these two terms were already distinguished "before Mencius's time."[15] The difference between the meaning of *xing* and that of *sheng,* however, varies according to specific contexts and philosophers. For the most part, it can be said that, although the connotation of *xing* does not exactly coincide with that of *sheng,* one covers a large part of the other.[16] Viewed from the above passage, which is at the beginning of Xunzi's discussion of names that belong to human beings in the chapter, "On the Proper Use of Names (*zhengminglun* 正名論)," it is likely that Xunzi employs *sheng* as the most basic biological feature in defining the notion of *xing.* In other words, Xunzi does not seem to confer any ethical dimension on *xing* by defining it in terms of *sheng.* Second, the language Xunzi uses to depict the way *xing* functions is very close to the expressions he uses to portray the way *tian* works.

Similar expressions that make clear *xing*'s direct connection to *tian* can be found in the following passage:

> *Xing* is that which is given by *tian;* you cannot learn it, you cannot acquire it by effort. . . . That part of man which cannot be learned or acquired by effort is called *xing.* (87/23/11–12, Knoblock 23.1c, Watson 158)

Spontaneity and effortlessness are characteristics that belong to *tian.* Considering that *tian* engenders human beings, it is not surprising that a human is born with qualities that share *tian*'s characteristics. What is important, however, is that those are not deterministic features that define humankind as humankind. In other words, although *xing* refers to the basic psychophysiological features with which a human is born, it cannot be regarded as an essential human nature that can distinguish humans from other beings; *xing,* for

Xunzi, refers to no more than "brute" facts about humans. Thus, Xunzi says: "Human *xing* is the root and beginning, the raw material and original constitution" (73/19/76, Knoblock 19.5b, Watson 102). This *xing* as the basis and raw material given by *tian* includes not only the faculties of sense organs but also the desire for food, clothing, rest, and so on.

> It is a part of man's *xing* that his eyes can see and his ears can hear. But the faculty of clear sight can never exist separately from the eyes, nor the faculty of keen hearing exist separately from the ear. (87/23/13–14, Knoblock 23.1d, Watson 159)
>
> Now it is man's *xing* that when he is hungry he will desire something to eat, when he is cold he will desire clothing, and when he is weary he will desire rest. (87/23/17–18, Knoblock 23.1e, Watson 159)

That the scope of *xing* includes the faculties of the sense organs as well as desires indicates that Xunzi views *xing* as not confined to some specific human faculties or instincts, but encompassing all the passively responsive human faculties that are given by *tian*.

Accordingly, emotional feelings are also defined in terms of *xing:*

> The feelings of liking and disliking, of delight and anger, and of sorrow and joy that are inborn in our *xing* are called "emotions (*qing* 情)." (83/22/3, Knoblock 22.1b)

At this point, we need to recall that Mencius directly connects human emotional dispositions with his claim that human *xing* is good (*Mencius* 6A:6). By contrast, Xunzi, although he also includes emotions as one of the components of *xing,* does not suggest that human emotional feelings have anything to do with the ethical character one should develop. Also noteworthy is that, while it is controversial in the *Mencius* whether the notion of *xin* can be clearly distinguished from that of *xing,* this problem does not occur for Xunzi. Xunzi explicitly distinguishes the faculty of *xin* from passively given, natural features, namely, *xing*. This characterization of *xing* as passively responsive human qualities that have no normative dimension paves the way for his provocative claim that human *xing* is bad.

The "Badness" of *Xing*

When Xunzi defines *xing* as something that is endowed by *tian* and cannot be learned or acquired by effort, it is in the context of criticizing Mencius:

> Mencius contended that "the fact that man is capable of learning implies that his *xing* is good."[17] I say that this is not so. It shows that Mencius did not reach any real understanding of what man's *xing* is and that he did not investigate the division between those things that are just given properties (*xing*) in humans and those that are acquired by deliberative activity. (*wei* 偽) (87/23/10–11, Knoblock 23.1c)

According to Xunzi, the claim that "human *xing* is good" does not follow from the fact that "man is capable of learning." Mencius's critical misunderstanding of the notion of *xing* leads him to neglect the most pivotal point in Confucianism: that goodness is achieved through human efforts, not passively given. Although it can be argued that Mencius located the concept of achievement in his notion of *xing*,[18] at least from Xunzi's perspective, Mencius could have been seen as not fully aware of the significance of the distinction between the given properties of human beings and achievement by deliberative exertion. For Xunzi, the most effective way of preventing this confusion is not to allow any concept of achievement in the notion of *xing*. After claiming that "it is human *xing* that when hungry he desires something to eat . . . that when weary he desires rest," Xunzi gives a dramatic example to support his argument for the division of *xing* and deliberative activity:

> But when in fact a man is hungry, if he sees one of his elders, he will not eat before his elder does; rather, he will defer to him. When he is weary from work, he does not presume to ask to be given rest time, for he realizes that he should relieve others. A son's deference to his father and a younger brother's deference to his elder brother; a son's relieving his father of work and a younger brother's relieving his elder brother—acts such as these are all contrary to one's *xing* and run counter to his emotions (*qing* 情). And yet they represent the way of filial piety and the proper forms of ritual and morality (*liyizhiwenli* 禮義之文理). Hence, if persons follow their *xing*, there will be no courtesy or humility (*cirang* 辭讓); courtesy and humility in fact run counter to a person's *xing*. From this it is obvious, then, that human *xing* is bad, and that his goodness is the result of deliberative activity (*wei*). (87/23/18–22, Knoblock 23.1e, Watson 159–160)

Given the importance of filial piety and brotherly deference in Confucian morality, Xunzi's claim that those virtues do not originate from *xing* as natural emotional propensities, but from deliberative activity, is indeed remarkable; in other words, Xunzi seems to thoroughly cut the tie with *tian* as the source for morality. Human morality is, thus, grounded upon deliberative effort, rather than *tian*-given natural propensities.[19]

His claim that human *xing* is bad, however, seems too extreme; it does not logically follow that *xing* cannot be the basis for human morality. Why did Xunzi repeatedly maintain throughout the chapter entitled "Human *xing* is Bad (*xinge*)" that human *xing* is bad, instead of saying that it is morally neutral? Let us consider one of Xunzi's more explicit descriptions about the badness of *xing:*

> Human *xing* is bad; any goodness is acquired by deliberative exertion (*wei*). Now, human *xing* is such that he is born with a love of profit (*li* 利). Following this *xing* will cause its aggressiveness and greedy tendencies to grow and courtesy and deference (*cirang*) to disappear. Humans are born with feelings of envy and hatred. Indulging these feelings causes violence and crime to develop and loyalty and trustworthiness (*zhongxin* 忠信) to perish. Man is born possessing the desires (*yu* 欲) of the ears and eyes. Indulging these desires causes dissolute and wanton behavior to result and rituals and morality (*liyi* 禮義), and good form and reasonableness (*wenli* 文理) to perish. (86/23/1–3, Knoblock 23.1a, Watson 157)

Here, human *xing* is depicted as human, incipient tendencies to seek profit, emotional feelings of envy and hatred, and the desires of the sense organs. If these tendencies inherent in human *xing* are allowed to grow without control, they become so destructive that moral virtues and culture necessary to sustain human society disappear and perish. In discussing the need for rituals in an orderly society, Xunzi specifically singles out human desires (*yu* 欲) as the inherent destructive propensities that bring about chaos and poverty:

> Men are born with desires which, if not satisfied, cannot but lead men to seek to satisfy them. If in seeking to satisfy their desires men observe no measure and apportion things without limits, then it would be impossible for them not to contend over the means to satisfy their desires. Such contention leads to disorder. Disorder leads to poverty. (70/19/1–2, Knoblock 19.1a)

The human desire for satisfaction is limitless; if there is no constraint on their gratification, they will quarrel with each other.

These two passages seem to support the literal interpretation of Xunzi's claim that human *xing* is bad. However, even though human *xing*, particularly emotions and desires, tends to be destructive, this does not confirm that these incipient tendencies are themselves bad. Take the example of a wild horse. Without a bridle it is likely to destroy fences and injure people, yet if it is well trained and controlled with a bridle, it could be a good horse. In this case, we do not say that the horse is bad; we just say that the horse has a tendency to be wild that can be controlled with proper training and a bridle. In addition, the way Xunzi defines the terms goodness and badness (*shane* 善惡) does not seem to invest each notion with its own respective independent, objective character. He defines goodness as "*zheng* 正 (what is correct), *li* 理 (reasonable, in accord with natural pattern), *ping* 平 (peaceful), and *zhi* 治 (well-ordered)" (88/23/37, Knoblock 23.3a), and badness in opposite terms as "*pian* 偏 (what is wrong through partiality), *xien* 險 (what contravenes reasonableness or natural pattern), *bei* 悖 (rebellious), and *luan* 亂 (chaotic)" (88/23/37, Knoblock 23.3a). Although *pian, xien, bei,* and *luan* have negative overtones, they are all relative to *zheng, li, ping,* and *zhi*. In other words, badness in Xunzi's philosophy is not "evil" existing independent of goodness. The degree of badness is decided relatively according to the degree to which the harmonious equilibrium in a society is broken down. In fact, when he condemns the contemporary rulers who "urgently pursue pleasure but are sluggish in putting their countries in order" (39/11/45, Knoblock 11.4), Xunzi does so not because they follow their desires; rather, he readily admits that the desires of the sensory organs are human emotional dispositions (*qing* 情) that cannot be avoided. He criticizes that these rulers gratify their desires without considering whether their countries are rich enough, whether they rule them in "a way that produces order and management, power and defensive strength" (39/11/48, Knoblock 11.4). A ruler who follows his *xing* is not to be condemned, so long as he does not indulge his desires excessively and he builds an orderly, prosperous society.

A substantial part of Xunzi's argument in the "Human *xing* is bad" chapter is devoted to establishing the contrast between the character of *xing* as the spontaneous disposition of human beings and the notion of *wei* as the source for rituals and morality. The following passage demonstrates this contrast between *xing* and *wei:*

> Phenomena such as the eye's fondness for beautiful forms, the ear's fondness for beautiful sounds, the mouth's fondness for delicious flavors, the *xin*'s fondness for profit,[20] or the body's fondness for pleasure and relaxation—these are all products of human *xing*. When there is stimulation (*gan* 感), they respond spontaneously (*zhiran* 自然). They do not require that a person first apply herself before they are produced. But what cannot be produced by such stimulation but rather must await application before it can be produced is called the result of deliberative activity (*wei*). These are the distinguishing characteristics that show that what is produced by deliberative activity is not the same as what is produced by the characteristics inherent in human *xing*. (87/23/25–27, Knoblock 23.2a)

Right after this passage, Xunzi goes on to say that the sage is one who can transform (*hua* 化) his *xing* and who initiates conscious activity. He is different from ordinary people, not in his *xing*, but in his deliberative exertion (*wei*). What is noteworthy is Xunzi's contention that *xing* is transformable. If he wanted to claim that *xing* is a part of fixed, human nature that consists of nothing but the tendency to be bad, Xunzi would not have described *xing* as something that can be transformed by the sage; he would rather have depicted it as something controllable by other human faculties such as *xin*, so that he could establish the clear dichotomy between the badness of *xing* and the goodness of deliberative activity. Instead, Xunzi returns to his more morally neutral definition of *xing*.

In light of the foregoing discussion, it would be more appropriate to interpret Xunzi's thesis of the badness of *xing* less literally. Xunzi's real intention is to argue that goodness is the result of deliberative activity. The repeated statements about the badness of human *xing* can be regarded as a calculated rhetorical device to attack the naturalists, who believe that goodness can be derived from following the spontaneity of nature or spontaneous emotional predispositions. The following remarks in the "Discourse on Ritual (*lilun*)" chapter on the complementary relation between *xing* and deliberative activity, without uttering any value judgments on the notion of *xing*, seem to represent Xunzi's basic idea of *xing* better than any passage in the "Human *xing* is bad" chapter:

> Therefore I say that human *xing* is the basis and raw material, and conscious activity is responsible for what is adorned, ordered, and flourishing. If there were no human *xing*, there would be nothing for conscious activity to work upon, and if there were no deliberative activity, then human *xing* would have no way to refine itself. Only after *xing* and deliberative exertion have been conjoined is the concept of the sage perfected and the merit of uniting the world brought to fulfillment. (73/19/75–77, Knoblock 19.6, Watson 102)

Here, *xing* and deliberative activity are depicted as being complementary to each other. *Xing* is no longer portrayed as a culprit that brings about chaos and disorder; it is raw material without which deliberative activity has nothing to work on. Only after deliberative activity works on *xing* properly, we can have the perfect concept of the sage and the merit of uniting the world can be brought into fulfillment.

We began our discussion on Xunzi's notion of *xing* with several questions: Does the implication of his claim that human *xing* is bad have anything to do with *tian?* Can *xing* be rendered as human nature? What is the *xing*'s relationship with *xin?* As has been shown, there seems to be some discrepancy between Xunzi's conception of *xing* and his claim that human *xing* is bad. In his definition of *xing*, Xunzi does not confer any normative dimension on it. That is, Xunzi treats *xing* as a descriptive term, referring to something inherent in humans that is given by *tian*. *Xing* functions spontaneously, without having to be learned. However, when he characterizes badness as something that destroys social norms and order, Xunzi ascribes it to human spontaneous predispositions, namely *xing*. Recalling that for Xunzi *tian*, though stripped of any specific normative implication, is still the object of awe, it is not at all likely that Xunzi intends to suggest that *tian* is the source of badness because of the badness of *xing*. It is more likely that Xunzi's basic idea of *xing* lies in his definitional approach to it as brute facts about humans. From this perspective, the reconstruction of his ideas on the notion of *xing* can be as follows: *xing* is neither good nor bad, it is just the psychophysiological features with which a person is born. Badness is itself a notion relative to goodness. If we govern and educate our inborn natural predispositions, they do us no harm. In fact, they are unavoidable features on which we should build our ethical norms and cultures. However, the naturalists such as Mencius and Zhuangzi do not understand the essential division between naturally given predispositions and deliberately exerted achievements. Particularly if we construe Mencius's claim that human *xing* is good as permission for humans to freely follow their spontaneous dispositional qualities, such as desires and emotions, we should firmly warn against those who follow Mencius. Human *xing* is not good. It is more likely to become destructive without deliberative exertion. The sage is someone who has no difference in his *xing*, but who educates and transforms his *xing* to refine his dispositional qualities and shape ethicocultural norms such as rituals.

Viewed from the standpoint of the above reconstruction, Xunzi's *xing* is not a predetermined nature. Although these dispositional tendencies given by *tian* can be destructive, they can be refined and transformed by conscious effort. Therefore, we should not literally accept Xunzi's thesis that human *xing* is bad. Accordingly, he does not imply that the source of badness is *tian*. *Tian* as the source of *xing* only seems to signify that, as we should not seek ethical orientation from *tian*, we should not expect *xing* to be good without deliberative activity. Then, from whence does deliberative activity arise? The only possible source that is not included in the contents of *xing* is *xin*. It is the portrayal of *xing* as the passively given qualities that highlights the active, autonomous faculty of *xin*.

Chapter 4

The Notion of *Xin* 心

Introduction

I have been arguing that Xunzi's philosophical anthropology is based on the distinction between passively responsive faculties represented by the conception of *xing* and the notion of *xin* as the active faculty of self-governance. Is Xunzi's characterization, particularly his notion of *xin* as the faculty of self-governance, unique in ancient Chinese philosophy? Does this conception of *xin* have any other features besides that of self-governance? First, I examine the evolution of the notion of *xin* to see whether Xunzi's notion is unique and, to determine why he characterizes it as the faculty of self-governance. Second, we will take a look at the largely ignored usage of *xin* in the *Xunzi,* that is, a usage that is more akin to the character of *xing* than to that of the autonomous *xin*. An answer is suggested to the question of why Xunzi allows the notion of *xin* to have such diverse implications. These preliminary sketches lay the groundwork for my exploration of the various aspects of *xin* as the faculty of self-governance.

The Evolution of the Notion of *Xin* in Ancient Chinese Philosophy

In the bronze inscriptions, the word *xin* appears as "a picture of the physical organ."[1] The *Shuo-wen* lexicon also confirms that *xin* is a human corporeal organ located in the middle of the body.[2] One of the reasons we avoid using *mind* as the translation of *xin* is because the term itself, even from its origin, denies the dichotomies of mind and body, and mind and emotions. This bodily organ seems mainly to have referred to the center of emotional feelings. In the *Book of Odes* (*Shijing*), which is regarded as one of the oldest extant documents, "dated between c. 1000 and c. 600 B.C.,"[3] *xin* is referred to on several occasions as something that expresses the various states of emotions and sentiments such as sorrow, anguish, distress, and love.[4] In these instances, we may render *xin* as "heart." However, in the poem entitled "Clever Words," where it reads, "The words of way-farers that come and go, / Can be discriminated by *xin*,"[5] and on other occasions, *xin* refers to "the source of intellect and understanding," or "the source of moral exertion,"[6] though less frequently than to the center of emotional feelings. This is where many commentators employ "mind" as the translation of *xin*. In the *Analects of Confucius*, a moral tone is added to this dual character of *xin*, particularly to its emotional aspect. It is "the seat of *ren* 仁 (humaneness, authenticity),"[7] which can be described as follows in addressing Yan Hui's character: "His *xin* would not go astray from *ren* for three months."[8] Confucius does not ascribe any ethical implications to the intellectual aspect of *xin;* it is portrayed as the brain or mind, which is employed in playing games such as chess.[9]

Among the texts dated close to or contemporary with Confucius, we find in the *Mozi* and the *Guanzi* that *xin* is used in significant ways. In the middle section of the "Identifying with One's Superior (*Shangtong* 上同)" chapter of the *Mozi*, there is an expression that the son of heaven (*tianzi* 天子) "makes others' *xin* to aid in his considered thinking (*silu* 思慮)."[10] This *xin* has views and plans by which to help the ruler possess a godlike intelligence.[11] In attacking Confucius, it is said, "What Kong Qiu 孔丘[12] did is the consequence of the way his *xin* had led."[13] Although there are passages in which *xin* refers to the seat of emotions, *xin* gradually gained significance in the *Mozi* as the thinking organ. Particularly in the so-called dialectic chapters dated around 2–3 B.C., we can see that *xin* is predominantly used to refer to the organ of intelligence. Considering that Xunzi's theory of names is heavily influenced by the Later Mohists' doctrine in the dialectic chapters,[14] it can be said that Xunzi, though criticizing the Mohists overtly, is not hesitant to adopt some aspects of Mohism in shaping his notion of *xin*.

Another important source for the evolution of the meaning of *xin* is the *Guanzi*. Considered to encompass "a wide mixture of material written by a number of unnamed writers over a long period of time,"[15] from the fifth century B.C. to the middle of the first century B.C.,[16] it contains diverse philosophical trends, including Confucianism, Daoism, and Legalism. In the "Inner Workings (*Neiye* 內業)" chapter, which is dated to the fourth or early third century B.C.,[17] we find three important ideas about the notion of *xin*.[18] The first is that *xin* is something that governs the sense organs: "When our *xin* are well regulated (*zhi* 治), our sense organs are also well governed. When our *xin* are at ease (*an* 安), our sense organs are also at ease. What governs them is *xin*. What sets them at ease is *xin*."[19] The second idea is that *xin*, which is a naturally given spontaneous faculty, can be perfected naturally unless it is disturbed by emotions and desires: "It is ever so that *xin*'s gestalt (*xing* 形) is naturally full and naturally replete, naturally born and naturally perfected. Should its function be impaired, it is certain to be due to sorrow and happiness, joy and anger, desire and profit seeking. If we can rid ourselves of sorrow and happiness, joy and anger, desire and profit seeking, *xin* will revert to its flawless state."[20] The third important idea is that within *xin* there is another *xin*: "*Xin* contains an inner *xin*. That is to say within *xin* there is another *xin*."[21]

The first idea of *xin* seems to have exerted a direct influence on Xunzi: the state of the sense organs, namely, sense perceptions, directly depends on the state of *xin* and thus we can say that *xin* regulates or governs (*zhi* 治) the sense organs. However, in the second idea, there are aspects in the character of *xin* that are not found in the *Xunzi;* although both Xunzi and Guanzi[22] share the idea that *xin* has a governing ability over the sense organs, Guanzi also claims that *xin* is something that is naturally given and naturally perfected. Thus, when it is said that this natural *xin*'s function can be impaired by emotions and desires, it is unclear how to distinguish between the governing *xin* and the natural *xin*. If *xin* is affected by emotions and desires, how can *xin* govern the sense organs? While the contention that within *xin* there is another *xin* seems to answer the question by suggesting a distinction between the natural *xin* and the governing *xin*,[23] there is no further articulation of it.

The notion of *xin*, which from its inception included both emotional and intellectual aspects, gained more implications as philosophical schools developed more sophisticated arguments concerning the source of morality and self-cultivation. In the *Mencius,* as we have already observed, *xin* is portrayed as having the faculties of both emotion and intellect; while, as an emotional faculty, *xin* is the source of morality, it is also the only organ that has the ability to think and judge what is right. However, it is not easy to see how Mencius reconciled these two aspects in the notion of *xin*. In other words, there seems to be an unbridgeable gap between the Mencian notion of *xin* as the spontaneous and emotional source of morality and as the cognitive and voluntary agent that guides our moral action.[24]

Zhuangzi attempted to establish the notion of *xin* as the center of Daoist self-cultivation. At the level of the achieved state, *xin* reflects the spontaneous way of nature without any distortion. One of the crucial steps to achieve this state of *xin* is to empty all judgmental thinking and emotional desires from *xin*. In this sense, it can be said that, since he does not regard either emotional or intellectual faculty as the significant function of *xin* for self-cultivation, Zhuangzi does not encounter the problem of reconciliation between the two aspects of *xin*. However, what is not clear in Zhuangzi's philosophy is how we are able to transform ordinary *xin* into achieved *xin;* insofar as voluntary, intellectual, and emotional features in the faculty of *xin* are regarded as obstacles to reaching achieved *xin,* the process of the transformation of ordinary *xin* into achieved *xin* appears quite mysterious.

Seen against the background of the evolution of the notion of *xin,* it is not difficult to notice that the autonomous feature in Xunzi's *xin* is not only unique in ancient Chinese philosophy, it is also significant in solving the problem of how to cultivate oneself. Without assuming the notion of autonomy as the primary feature of *xin,* all the attempts to give a cogent explanation regarding the unity of *xin* as the agent of self-cultivation seem to have failed. In the *Guanzi, xin* was described as something that can govern the senses, and can, at the same time, be disturbed by emotions and desires. In the *Mencius, xin* as the emotional source for morality was also taken to be the agent that leads to one's self-cultivation. In the *Zhuangzi,* the way to reach the achieved state of *xin* remained a puzzle. With the notion of the autonomy of *xin,* Xunzi could establish *xin* as the agent of self-cultivation that leads the senses, emotions, and desires in a proper direction. As I demonstrate in the next section, it is also the autonomous faculty as the foremost feature of *xin* that allows *xin* to be comprehensively characterized as the seat of all psychological phenomena—not only emotions and desires, but also intellect and volition—without much difficulty in assuming its unity.

The Customary Usage of *Xin* in the *Xunzi*

Until now, the notion of *xin* in the *Xunzi* has been described almost exclusively as the faculty of self-governance. However, if we look at the whole book of *Xunzi,* we find that numerous expressions in which *xin* is used in different ways. In fact, with the exception of a few chapters—the "Discourse on *Tian* 天," "Discourse on *Li* 禮," "On the Proper Use of Names (*zhengming* 正名)," and "Dispelling Blindness (*jiebi* 解蔽),"—we hardly find any reference to *xin* as the faculty of self-governance.[25] How can this be explained? One easy answer would be that Xunzi divides the uses of *xin* in two: *xin* as the faculty of self-governance was employed in a technical, philosophical sense, and in the other cases it was used in nontechnical, ordinary ways that had currency in the late Warring States period. Some arguments can be offered for this explanation; as most commentators on Xunzi have agreed, the chapters in which *xin* is defined as the faculty of self-governance are the most philosophically significant. In these chapters, Xunzi elaborates his major philosophical concepts, such as *xin, xing, li, tian,* and names. In other chapters, Xunzi gives scarcely any clear expositions of these terms. However, the problem with this explanation is that, while there is not much discrepancy in the meanings of other philosophical terms between the philosophical and nonphilosophical chapters, there is a clear difference in the implication of *xin* in these two parts of the book. Granted, more than four-fifths of the uses of *xin* can be understood in a nontechnical sense, but there is need for a fuller explanation as to why Xunzi allows *xin* to have such different implications.

First, it is important to recall that, when dealing with the dualistic aspects of *tian*, *xin*, both as the *tian*-endowed physical organ and the faculty of self-governance, is the key to the understanding of dualistic *tian*. Accordingly, it is evident that Xunzi's unique contribution to the evolution of the notion of *xin*—his characterization of *xin* as the faculty of self-governance—does not mean that he rejects the aspect of the *tian*-endowed bodily organ in *xin*. Bearing this in mind, let us look at the expressions in which *xin* lacks the characteristic of self-governance: Xunzi refers to *xin* as "profit-seeking one" (17/6/37, Knoblock 6.11), "comfort-desiring one" (39/11/46, Knoblock 11.4), "having resentment and ill will in it" (19/7/34, Knoblock 7.4), "a scoundrel's *xin*" (19/7/34, Knoblock 7.5), "a deceptive *xin*" (38/11/21, Knoblock 11.1d). The descriptions of *xin* as something that seeks profit, desires comfort, has resentment and ill will in it, deceives, and is possessed by a scoundrel, all point to the established usage of *xin* as the seat of emotions, desires, and intellect. These expressions are surprisingly similar to Xunzi's negative descriptions of the characteristics of *xing*. From this we can infer that the notion of *xin* as the bodily organ given by *tian* is almost identical with the well-established meaning of *xin* as the seat of emotions, desires, and intellect. It also shares the characteristics in the notion of *xing* that refer to the natural tendencies given by *tian*. Thus, it is not that Xunzi employs the notion of *xin* in an inconsistent manner; rather, since his notion of *xin* encompasses both the meaning of the faculty of self-governance and that of the bodily organ, which is the referential point for the passively responsive psychological phenomena, he uses various meanings of *xin* depending on the specific contexts.

Xunzi's theory of names supports this interpretation. In the chapter "On the Proper Use of Names," although he holds a conventionalist position regarding the invention of names, Xunzi insists on respecting established terms; without careful considerations of given circumstances, to invent new terms or revise established usages would lead to a more chaotic situation.[26] Accordingly, Xunzi must have been very careful in adding a new meaning to the notion of *xin*. His main concern was not to redefine *xin* in a completely novel way, but to add a key philosophical feature to it. It is thus not remarkable that, except for some specific philosophical contexts in which the feature of self-governance in *xin* is emphasized, Xunzi freely employs the established meaning of *xin*, which can be rendered as the seat of desires and emotions.

Noteworthy and pertinent to the notion of *xin* having the characteristics of both *xing* and self-governance is that it can offer a clue to the problem of the interpretation of the so-called ladder passage:

> Water and fire have energy (*qi* 氣) but are without life (*sheng* 生). Grass and trees have life but are without consciousness (*zhi* 知). Birds and beasts have consciousness but are without a sense of appropriateness (*yi* 義). Humans have energy, life, consciousness, and in addition, a sense of appropriateness. Therefore they are the noblest beings on earth. They are not as strong as the ox, not as swift as the horse, and yet they make the ox and the horse work for them. Why? I say humans are able to organize themselves in society and animals are not able to organize themselves in society. How are humans able to form societies (*qun* 群)? I say it is due to the social distinctions (*fen* 分). How do social divisions work? I say it is because of humans' sense of appropriateness. Bringing their sense of appropriateness to bear on these social distinctions results in a harmonious society (*he* 和). (28–29/9/69–71, Knoblock 9.16a)

The problem here is how to relate the assertion that "the sense of appropriateness" is the essential feature that separates human beings from beasts to Xunzi's claim that human *xing* is bad. From the standpoint of our arguments that his claim of the badness of *xing* is intentionally exaggerated for the purpose of attacking the naturalists and that his notion of *xing* should be construed as referring to morally neutral "brute facts" about humans instead of human nature, because it does not refer to essential features that separate humans from other beings, half of the problem seems to have already been solved. The remaining half, then, is where to locate "the sense of appropriateness" in Xunzi's philosophy. The notion of *xing* was construed, not as essential nature, but as natural tendencies that do not distinguish humans from other beings. It is therefore important to look for another candidate that may contain the sense of appropriateness—not just a morally neutral faculty but a positive sense that makes humans "the noblest beings on earth."

In light of the foregoing analysis of the notion of *xin,* which is characterized as having the faculty of self-governance and, at the same time, refers to the seat of all psychological phenomena, it seems reasonable to assume that the sense of appropriateness is regarded as one of the properties of *xin*. We can give the following argument for this interpretation: first, because *xin* also contains *xing*-like natural tendencies, it is likely that Xunzi regards the sense of appropriateness as one of the natural dispositions of *xin*. However, this does not mean that it is necessarily an emotional disposition that has its own direction; rather, it seems much closer to an instinctive awareness or consciousness through which a person learns to see and grasp things. It is, on the one hand, a sense or a feeling inherent in human beings, and, on the other, an intuitive capability by which to gain knowledge of the distinctions necessary for building a society. In this view, the sense of appropriateness can be categorized as both a natural, psychological disposition and a self-reflective disposition that leads humans to see that they are social animals. It can also be seen as a sense of morality, as the awareness of humans as social beings requires humans to make social distinctions in order to form a harmonious society. Accordingly, this "intuitive moral sense" seems to be the fundamental basis on which *xin* as the faculty of self-governance is able to control unruly tendencies inherent in humans and thus develop a harmonious society.[27]

Thus, Xunzi's use of *xin* in the ordinary sense does not conflict with his use of *xin* as the faculty of self-governance. Unlike those who appear to have held a two-level theory of *xin,* notably Guanzi and Mencius, Xunzi seems to have incorporated his notion of *xin* as the faculty of self-governance into the established usage of *xin* without much tension. In his notion of *xin,* the manifestation of *xin* as the bodily organ, which is the seat of all psychological phenomena including the senses, emotions, and desires, depends on its faculty of self-governance. If *xin* works properly as the faculty of self-governance, the unruly tendencies of emotions and desires can be transformed and serve as a basis for self-cultivation and an orderly society. Further, the sense of appropriateness as the defining feature and one of the natural dispositions of human beings can be encompassed by the comprehensive properties of *xin.* If the character of *xin* is strictly confined to the regulatory and autonomous function, there would be no place for the notion of the sense of appropriateness in the spectrum of Xunzian moral psychology.

It seems opportune at this point to review the foregoing discussions surrounding Xunzi's notion of the "autonomy" of *xin.* It was suggested that the autonomous character in Xunzi's notion of *xin* is crucial in comprehending his apparently contradictory claims of the conventionality of human morality, on the one hand, and of its "objectivity," based upon natural order, on the other. To understand Xunzi's notion of autonomous *xin* demanded an examination of the philosophical background against which he had developed it. Because ancient Chinese naturalism, which holds either spontaneous emotions as the source of morality or natural spontaneity itself as the ultimate way of life for humans, seems to have been the foremost concern for Xunzi, I examined two philosophers whom Xunzi was most likely to consider to represent naturalism: the Confucian naturalist Mencius, and the Daoist naturalist Zhuangzi. From this, I demonstrated that the distinction between the notions of *xing* and *xin* and the conception of *tian* are pivotal in understanding the distinctive character of *xin* in Xunzi's philosophical system. Through the examination of *tian* in Xunzi's philosophy, I observed that the dualistic aspects of *tian,* which works independently of human affairs on the one hand, and serves as the ultimate aspirational end for human moral effort on the other, is closely linked to the notion of *xin* that is given by *tian* and also has the faculty of self-governance. In discussing Xunzi's notion of *xing,* I showed that by strictly confining the notion of *xing* to the passively responsive properties in humans, Xunzi clearly distinguishes it from *xin.*

In this chapter, I first dealt with the evolution of the meaning of *xin.* The investigation of the evolution of *xin* leads me to conclude that, although Xunzi adopts several features of *xin* from previous and contemporary usages, the autonomy of *xin* is Xunzi's unique strategy to cope with the problem of self-cultivation, that is, how *xin* as the agent of cultivation can direct and supervise the disruptive tendencies of desires and emotions that have generally been regarded as the manifestations of *xin.* By ascribing the autonomous ability to *xin,* Xunzi renders *xin* able to supervise the sense organ, emotions, and desires without assuming another *xin.* Xunzi's notion of the autonomy of *xin* was the outcome of his general concern with naturalism and also his solution to the specific problem of self-cultivation. However, an indexical examination of the usages of *xin* in the *Xunzi* revealed that there are many examples that do not refer to *xin* as the faculty of self-governance. I proffered several explanations: first, it seems that Xunzi has two uses of *xin,* the technical, philosophical usage and the nontechnical, ordinary usage. Second, given his linguistic conservatism, Xunzi seems to have been very careful in adding a new meaning to the notion of *xin.* Thus, except for philosophically relevant passages, Xunzi does not attempt to revise the established usage of *xin,* and he does not intend to invent a new term for his purposes. Third and most important, the common use of *xin* implied that it was a bodily organ, with features characteristic of *xing.* In other words, as far as *xin* refers to a physical organ, it cannot but entail passively responsive qualities. Accepting this ordinary sense of *xin,* however, allows Xunzi to include the notion of sense of appropriateness (*yi* 義) in the content of *xin.* Different from spontaneous moral emotions, this sense of appropriateness offers a fitting basis on which the autonomous *xin* can exercise deliberate effort. The sense of appropriateness should not be seen as a spontaneous feeling or emotion that does not need deliberation and conscious effort, like a commiserating mind that cannot bear seeing a child fall into a well;[28] it should be seen as an incipient, intuitive sense that must await cognitive and volitional efforts to be actualized.

In short, in Xunzi's philosophy, while human morality retains a tenuous connection with *tian,* because it is *tian* that endows the sense of appropriateness inherent in humans, morality is also a human construction, because the development of the sense of appropriateness relies on the exertion of a person's intellect and volition.

Xin as the Faculty of Self-Governance

When Xunzi characterizes *xin* as "the lord given by *tian* (*tianjun* 天君)," he implies that, while *xin* is one of the *tian*-given organs, it is different from other, passively responsive faculties because it is in active supervision over them:

> When the work of *tian* has been established and its achievements perfected, the physical form (*xing* 形) becomes whole and the spirit (*shen* 神)[29] is born. Love and hate, delight and anger, sorrow and joy, are stored within—these are described as "the natural emotions (*tianqing* 天情)." The eye, ear, nose, mouth, and body each has what it is responsive to and they cannot interchange them—these are termed "the natural faculties (*tianguan* 天官)." *Xin* that dwells within the central cavity is used to control the five faculties—it is called "the lord provided by *tian*." (62/17/10–12, Knoblock 17.3a)

As the source of all myriad things, *tian* works in a spontaneous way and produces physical form and spirit. These two elements are combined and a person is born. Thus, all faculties in humans are given by *tian*. However, *xin* has a unique ability to govern the other faculties: the sense organs as well as the emotions and desires. As Xunzi puts it, *xin* is able to "choose among emotions" (83/22/3, Knoblock 22.1b), to accept what it thinks right (80/21/46, Knoblock 21.6a), and to approve or disapprove desires (85/22/57–60, Knoblock 22.5a). Although *xin* is the place in which sense perception, emotions, and desires all occur, it also has the higher function of leading them in the proper direction. Earlier, I called this aspect in the Xunzian notion of *xin* "the autonomy of *xin*." However, there is a need to further explicate this autonomous *xin:* On what basis does *xin* make its judgments and decisions? What is meant by the claim that *xin* "chooses" among emotions? What is *xin*'s relation to desires? Given its corporeality, how can *xin* be free from the influence of the sense organs, emotions, and desires? What is the achieved state of *xin* for Xunzi? To answer these questions, I scrutinize one of the most important passages regarding Xunzi's moral psychology. This provides an opportunity to expound on *xin*'s autonomous function of discerning and choosing among emotions, and to explore *xin*'s relation to the sense organs in Xunzi's moral epistemology.

Critical Thinking and Empirical Knowledge

The notion of autonomy as "the actual psychological condition of self-government"[30] presupposes a division between desires or emotions and critical reason. This is clear in the following definition of autonomy given by a contemporary Anglophone philosopher, Andrews Reath:

> [A]utonomy may be defined as the capacity to assess critically one's basic desires and values, to revise them if one judges that there is reason to, and to act on those that one identifies with or endorses upon critical reflection. This capacity enables one to take responsibility for one's basic desires and values, and to shape the direction of one's life. This definition relies on a distinction between first-order desires (desires for certain objects or activities) and higher-order reflection about one's first-order desires, and makes the capacity for higher-order critical reflection central to autonomy. Higher-order values may be viewed as judgments about which of one's first-order desires and values one wants to be moved by; or alternatively, as evaluative judgments as to whether goals or activities toward which one is inclined are really worth pursuing, whether certain of one's values or character traits are good, and so on.[31]

Although Xunzi does not use any term that can be translated as "autonomy" or give a systematic articulation of the notion of autonomy, there is a surprising similarity between the above, contemporary definition of autonomy and Xunzi's underlying idea of *xin*. The primary function of *xin*, for Xunzi, is critical or reflective thinking, which assesses and guides emotions and desires. We should, however, be wary of taking the distinction between first-order emotions or desires and higher-order critical reflection in Xunzi's philosophy as an ontological dichotomy between reason and emotion or desire. As *xin* does not refer to the abstract faculty separable from the body in Xunzi's philosophy, critical reasoning or thinking is not performed completely independent of emotions and desires. Xunzi's sage is also someone who "can follow his *xin*'s desire without overstepping the boundaries."[32] As A. S. Cua has pointed out, it seems more appropriate to adopt a functional interpretation of the distinction between the two; while the senses, emotions, and desires belong to bodily functions, critical reasoning and volition can be deemed mental functions.[33] Here, our attention should be given to Xunzi's articulation of *xin* as including higher-order critical reflection, which makes his moral psychology distinctive among ancient Chinese philosophers.

In the following passage, subtitled "the various names for what is within persons," Xunzi defines "deliberation (*lu* 慮)" and "deliberative exertion (*wei* 偽)" in terms of *xin*. This passage deserves careful analysis, because it offers both a synoptic view of Xunzi's moral psychology and a clue for exploring the epistemological issue regarding *xin*'s relation to sense perception:

> The feelings of liking and disliking, of delight and anger, and of sorrow and joy that are inborn in our *xing* are called "emotions (*qing* 情)." The emotions being so paired, the *xin*'s choosing between them is called "deliberation (*lu* 慮)." The *xin*'s thinking something and the ability to act upon it (*nengweizhidong* 能為之動) is called "deliberative exertion (*wei* 偽)." When thoughts are accumulated (*ji* 積) and one's natural abilities (*neng* 能)[34] have been exercised (*xi* 習) so that something is completed, it is called "deliberative exertion." (83/22/2–3, Knoblock 22.1b)

This passage follows the characterization of *xing* as something that is given from birth and works spontaneously by passively responding to external stimuli. After defining emotions in terms of *xing*, Xunzi introduces the notion of "deliberation (*lu* 慮)" as the activity of *xin* in choosing between bipolar pairs of emotions. At first, it appears odd that choosing an emotion is deemed an important part of critical thinking. However, it does not take long to understand Xunzi's thinking if we consider the following example: When we see someone slip and fall on icy ground, we tend to laugh without thinking of his or her pain. Once we put ourselves in his or her shoes, we stop laughing and worry about his or her condition. This process of thinking, which discerns one's emotional state and chooses the proper one, is the crucial part of critical reasoning that constitutes the autonomous function of *xin*. In another passage, Xunzi ascribes to *xin* not only the function of selection between emotions but also an ability to differentiate emotions and desires: "Pleasure and anger, sorrow and joy, love and hate, and desire are differentiated by *xin*" (83/22/18–19, Knoblock 22.2d).

The process of thinking that discerns and chooses between the various sets of emotions and desires is the pivotal juncture in Xunzi's moral psychology.[35] It is shown here that *xin* can be distinguished from other passively given faculties, because it is the thinking organ that leads an agent to follow the proper course of action by selecting an appropriate emotion or desire. Xunzi calls the resultant action "deliberative exertion (*wei* 偽)." It seems worth citing Knoblock's insightful analysis of the implication of the notion of deliberative exertion:

> This word [*wei* 偽] derives from L**gwjar*/S**wjaj* > *wei* 為 do, act, and naturally implies that exertion of the will is required in order to perform the act involved. It is thus the opposite of what is natural, in the sense of spontaneous (*ziran* 自然) actions a person performs without "deciding" or "willing" to do so.[36]

When I analyzed Xunzi's thesis that human *xing* is bad, I showed that his argument is based on the distinction between the notion of *xing* as passively given properties and that of deliberative exertion as the achievement of voluntary human efforts. Knoblock confirms this: The concept of deliberative exertion as voluntary and volitional actions or achievements entailed by *xin*'s thinking is intentionally devised to highlight its contrast to the natural and spontaneous actions to which natural tendencies lead. Thus, it is understandable that the notions of accumulation (*ji* 積) and exercise or repeated practice (*xi* 習) are prominent in the following other definition of deliberative exertion. One instance of thinking what is right and choosing the proper course of action does not guarantee the complete transformation of natural tendencies. Critical reflection is required on every occasion. It is also important that the faculties of the sense organs produce correct sensory data through numerous applications, because such data are the basic material through which *xin* gains genuine knowledge of things and puts it into practice. Accumulation and practice are what make the difference between the sage and ordinary people: "A person in the street, one of the Hundred Clans, who accumulated goodness and achieves it completely is called a sage. . . . Thus, becoming a sage is the result of what a man accumulated" (25/8/112–113, Knoblock 8.11).

As shown above, Xunzi asserts that the sense organs also need practice because the sensory data they produce are the basis on which *xin* acquires knowledge. This statement needs further explanation: What does it mean that one's natural abilities—namely, the sense organs—require practice for the completion of something, and how can they serve as the basis on which *xin* gains knowledge?

Xunzi's epistemological emphasis is that knowledge is gained through the combination of objective facts and subjective cognitive function. According to Xunzi, all persons have "the inherent means of knowing," called "awareness or consciousness (*zhi* 知)," and "knowledge (*zhi* 智)" is produced out of "awareness' tallying with the facts" (83/22/5, Knoblock 22.1b). Remember that, when pointing to the sense of appropriateness as the defining feature of human beings, Xunzi regards "awareness" as a characteristic that humans and animals share (29/9/69–70, Knoblock 9.16a). That is, awareness is closer to instinctive sense perception than it is to the function of critical reasoning and is merely the means by which humans, specifically human *xin*, attain knowledge.[37] What, then, are the content of awareness or perception and the role of *xin* in acquiring knowledge?

According to Xunzi, the basic function of awareness is the recognition of the sameness and difference among things or among perceptual states perceived by the sense organs. On the sameness of things, Xunzi observes: "As a general rule, whenever things belong to the same category (*tonglei* 同類) of being or have the same characteristics, the representation of them presented by the senses is the same" (83/22/16, Knoblock 22.2c). On the difference among sensory objects as well as among perceptual states, Xunzi more specifically expounds on the faculties of the sense organs:

> Forms, colors, and designs are differentiated by the eye. Pitch and timbre, bass and treble, modal keys and rhythm, and odd noises are differentiated by the ear. Sweet and bitter, salty and bland, pungent and sour, and distinctive tastes are differentiated by the mouth. Fragrance and stenches, perfumes and rotten odors, putrid and rancid smells, foul and sour odors, and distinctive strange smells are differentiated by the nose. Pain and itching, cold and heat, smoothness and roughness, and lightness and heaviness are differentiated by the body. (83/22/17–18, Knoblock 22.2d)

The problem with sense perception is that it is often mistaken and misleading. Although there would be no knowledge without the function of the sense organs that perceive both internal psychological states and external things, it alone seems not sufficient to confirm the validity of knowledge. Xunzi again relies on the notion of *xin* in solving the problem. According to him, *xin* has the ability to confirm the empirical knowledge given by the sense organs.[38] He calls this function of *xin* "*zhengzhi* 徵知":

> *Xin* has *zhengzhi*. Because of *zhengzhi,* it may rely upon the ear for recognizing sounds, the eye for recognizing forms. But before *zhengzhi* can be performed, it must wait for the senses to be impressed by the type of things to which sense organ [is sensitive]. (83/22/19–20, Knoblock 22.2e)

After all, the agent who knows something through perception is not the sense organs themselves; it is *xin*. Thus, whether we can avoid the pitfalls generated by the sense organs depends on whether *xin* has the ability to guard against them. Xunzi maintains that *xin* has "the confirmatory function with respect to knowledge,"[39] and also that the final step in gaining knowledge ultimately depends on *xin:*

> When *xin* is not employed (*xinbushiyen* 心不使焉), then although black and white are in front of a person's own eyes, he will not see them, or although the thunder drums are sounding on either side of him, his ears will not hear them. (78/21/4–5, Knoblock 21.1)

Without the active involvement of *xin*, we cannot even recognize what we are seeing and what we are hearing. This seems to have been in Xunzi's mind when he dubbed *xin* "the lord given by *tian*," which governs the faculties of the sense organs. However, we should not neglect the equal emphasis Xunzi places on the empirical source of knowledge. Without things that are white and black, *xin* cannot play a confirmatory role or gain any knowledge.

Now it is possible to provide a plausible interpretation of the notion of the exercise of the sense organs. Given Xunzi's emphasis on *xin*'s supervisory function over the sense organs and its confirmatory role in judging the empirical knowledge given by the sense organs, it seems appropriate that what Xunzi really means by the exercise of the sense organs is, in fact, the exercise of *xin*. Let us look again at the passage: "When thoughts are accumulated (*ji* 積) and one's natural abilities (*neng* 能) have been exercised (*xi* 習) so that something is completed, it is called conscious exertion." The agent that accumulates thoughts and trains the sense organs is *xin*. However, strictly speaking, the sense organs themselves cannot be trained: "Now, it belongs to human *xing* that the eye is able to see and the ear to hear. The ability to see clearly cannot be separated from the eye, nor the ability to hear acutely from the ear. It is quite impossible to learn to be clear-sighted or keen of hearing" (87/23/13–14, Knoblock 23.1d). Therefore, it is not the sense organs themselves that are trained, but the faculty of *xin*, which employs sense data in producing correct judgments, is "practiced." It is the proper use of the faculty of *xin* that enables us to correctly assess the empirical knowledge given by the sense organs and achieve culture and morality.

Our examination of the exercise of the sense organs gave us an opportunity to see how Xunzi establishes his epistemology. With Xunzi's emphasis on the normative function of knowledge as a guide to choosing a proper direction, it may be more appropriate to call his investigation of knowledge moral epistemology. In Xunzi's moral epistemology, the faculty of *xin* and empirical knowledge occupy central positions. While knowledge is produced by our experience, it is neither available nor reliable without the faculty of *xin*. The autonomous *xin*, which performs critical reflection on given emotions and desires and also validates empirical knowledge, can be characterized as the psychological agent that constantly guards against natural propensities, that is, the destructive tendencies of emotional desires and the deceptive inclinations of the sense organs.

Xunzi's epistemological investigation is comparable only to that of the Mohist school[40] in ancient Chinese philosophy, in which epistemological questions were largely overshadowed by the problems of self-cultivation. Early Chinese philosophers mainly concerned themselves with how we ought to cultivate ourselves to be the sages who embody the unity of knowledge and practice, rather than with how we acquire and justify knowledge. If we cultivate ourselves to the level of a sage, we comprehend things intuitively. Although Xunzi does not reject the notion of sagehood, he does not neglect epistemological questions altogether. Xunzi places stress on human autonomous morality that relies on deliberative exertion based on learning and efforts, rather than spontaneous and natural tendencies, and this understanding prompted him to explore the empirical ground of knowledge. Neither knowledge of things nor moral knowledge are just given; they are acquired through direct or indirect experiences that call for confirmation by the faculty of *xin*. From the standpoint of Xunzi's concern with the naturalism of his time, it also seems clear that his emphasis on the function of *xin* and the empirical source of knowledge targeted specific notions, such as the Mencian notions of "genuine ability (*liangneng* 良能)" and "genuine understanding (*liangzhi* 良知)":

> What persons are able to do without having to learn it is what they can truly do (*liangneng*); what persons know without having to reflect on it (*lu* 慮) is what they truly know (*liangzhi*). There are no young children who do not know loving their parents, and none of them when they grow up will not know respect for their elder brothers. Loving one's parents is humaneness (*ren* 仁); respecting one's elders is appropriateness (*yi* 義). What is left to be done is simply the extension of these to the whole Empire.[41]

It is noteworthy that neo-Confucians interpreted "*liang* 良" as "innate." Particularly, Wang Yangming's criticism of one of Zhu Xi's central tenets[42] that "the perfection of knowledge depends on the investigation of things (*gewu* 格物)"[43] is based on the notion of the "innateness 良" of moral knowledge. According to Wang Yangming, considered a genuine heir to Mencius, Zhu Xi does not understand that the source of moral knowledge must be sought within, rather than outside of, ourselves. Thus, it is not surprising that Xunzi takes epistemological exploration seriously as the foundation for an autonomous morality, instead of endorsing a naturalistic interpretation of morality.

In short, the autonomy of *xin* in Xunzi's philosophy is understood to be capable of choosing among emotions and desires and confirming knowledge given by the sense organs. In other words, Xunzi ascribes to *xin* "the faculty of critical reasoning" against given emotions and desires as well as "the confirmatory function" with regard to knowledge. In order to perform its function properly, *xin* needs accumulative practice, because natural human propensities of emotions, desires, and the sense organs tend to be misleading and destructive when *xin* ceases its proper function of guiding and authenticating them. Xunzi emphasizes *xin*'s confirmatory role particularly with regard to the sense organs. While the sense organs provide the basic material for acquiring knowledge, without the proper use of *xin,* we cannot confirm or even recognize the information. A. S. Cua calls Xunzi's emphasis on both the proper function of *xin* and experience in acquiring knowledge "concrete rationality."[44] It clearly differs from the Mencian approach to knowledge, which is based on the notion of "*liangzhi* 良知," interpreted by neo-Confucians as "innate moral knowledge."

Based on this overview of the notion of the autonomy of *xin,* I will take a closer look at the volitional aspect of *xin*. Issuing commands and approving or disapproving emotions and desires constitute the basic components of the notion of autonomy of *xin* in Xunzi. Xunzi's articulation of this volitional aspect of *xin* is also one of the characteristics that distinguishes him from other ancient Chinese philosophers.

The Volitional Aspect of *Xin*

A discussion of critical thinking as a central element in the notion of the autonomy of *xin* should not ignore that it is inseparable from the notion of the volitional capability of *xin*. In other words, for *xin* to perform critical thinking, it must have a volitional power that allows thinking to be unaffected or impaired by desires and emotions. The following passage is one of the most explicit statements made by Xunzi concerning the volitional capability of *xin:*

> *Xin* is the lord of the body (*xingzhijun* 形之君) and master of the spiritual intelligence (*shenmingzhizhu* 神明之主). It issues commands but does not receive commands. On its own authority it forbids or orders, renounces or selects, initiates or stops. Thus, the mouth can be forced to be silent or to speak. The body can be forced to crouch down or stretch out. But *xin* cannot be forced to change its ideas. If *xin* thinks something right (*shizhi* 是之), it will accept it; but if it thinks something wrong (*feizhi* 非之), then it will reject it. Therefore, it is said that the state of *xin* is such that of necessity it perceives on its own. No prohibitions can be placed on what it selects. Its objects are diverse and extensive. When it has perfect concentration, it is not divided in purpose. (80/21/44–47, Knoblock 21.6a)

In contrast to the notion of *xing* that refers to passively given natural tendencies, *xin* is here portrayed as the supreme commander, with complete independence in making decisions. It follows its own judgments and makes a person act on them. The decisions are based solely on *xin*'s judgment of what is right. This volitional aspect of *xin* is crucial in separating Xunzi from other philosophers, such as Guanzi and Mencius. Neither Guanzi's two-*xin* theory, which distinguishes between natural *xin* and governing *xin,* nor Mencius' notion of *xin,* which emphasizes both the spontaneous, emotional aspect of *xin* as the source of morality and the conscious and deliberative aspect of *xin* as the agent for self-cultivation, articulates the volitional aspect of *xin*. For this reason, Guanzi and Mencius cannot escape criticism with regard to the unity of *xin*.

In contrast, Xunzi's notion of the autonomy of *xin* highlights the volitional aspect of *xin*. Thus, while his notion of *xin* encompasses all psychological features, it avoids the confusion generated by its comprehensiveness; for all of the qualities of *xin* as a bodily organ are subjected to its intellectual and volitional execution. In other words, whether qualities such as emotions and desires can serve as the basis for deliberative exertion or as obstacles to it depends on how *xin* performs its reflective thinking with its autonomous volition. This is most remarkably shown in the following passage, where *xin* is depicted as the ultimate arbitrator in approving or disapproving desires:

> Desire does not depend on the object of desire first being obtainable, but what is sought follows upon what is approved of (*suoke* 所可).[45] That the occurrence of desire does not depend on its object's first being obtainable is a quality we receive from *tian*. That what is sought follows upon what is approved of is received from *xin*. (85/22/57–58, Knoblock 22.5a)

The hierarchical structure of *xin* allows emotions and desires, volition and intellect to coexist within the unity of *xin*. However insatiable the desires are by nature, they must await *xin*'s approval to be acted on.

Xunzi uses the radical example of life and death to underscore the volitional capability of *xin* in dictating the desires:

> What persons desire most is life, and what they hate most is death. Be that as it may, persons sometimes follow the pursuit of life and end up with death. It is not that they do not really desire life and rather desire death; it is that it was improper (*bukeyi* 不可以) to live and it was proper (*keyi* 可以) to die. Thus, when desires run to excess, actions do not reach that point because *xin* stops them. If what *xin* permits coincides with what is reasonable (*li* 理), then although the desires are numerous, how could there be harm to order (*zhi* 治)! Although the desires are not strong enough to motivate a person, his actions may exceed his desires because *xin* has ordered them to do so. If what *xin* permits conflicts with what is reasonable, then although the desires are few, how could it stop at disorder! Thus, order

> and disorder lie in what *xin* permits and not with the desires that belong to our natural dispositions (*qing* 情). Although you may claim to have success in finding the cause of order and disorder, if you do not seek it where it lies but instead seek it where it does not lie, then you will miss the truth. (85/22/59–63, Knoblock 22.5a)

The above statement is Xunzi's response to those who hold that "order requires that we first rid ourselves of desires"[46] and those who maintain that "order requires that first we reduce the number of our desires."[47] According to Xunzi, neither doctrine comprehends that the desires themselves are not the cause of disorder. *Xin* governs the desires, and the order of society, therefore, hinges on how properly *xin* does so. It will be valuable in elucidating Xunzi's view on the relationship between *xin* and desire if we compare the above passage with the way Mencius discusses life and death in relation to the desires.[48] Mencius first takes the example of appetite, saying that, although he wants both fish and bear's palm, if he has to choose one, he would take bear's palm because he wants it more than fish. He goes on to say,

> Life is what I want; appropriateness (*yi* 義) is also what I want. If I cannot have both, I would rather take appropriateness than life. On the one hand, though life is what I want, there is something I want more than life. That is why I do not cling to life at all costs. On the other hand, though death is what I hate, there is something I hate more than death. That is why there are troubles I do not avoid.[49]

Mencius attributes this quality of desire to *xin:* "It is not the case that only the moral person (*xianzhe* 賢者) has this *xin*. All humans have it. The moral person simply never loses it."[50] The difference between Xunzi and Mencius is striking; Mencius does not sharply distinguish *xin* from the desires. Persons desire morality most, rather than life. This urge for morality originates from *xin*. In other words, it is *xin* that desires morality. The moral person is someone who simply does not lose *xin*'s moral urge. In contrast, for Xunzi, the higher function of *xin* is distinct from first-order desires. Desire is given by *tian* and spontaneously seeks the object of desire, regardless of what the object is. However, it is the reflective and volitional *xin* that approves or disapproves the desires. Therefore, even though people desire life most and hate death most, they can choose death rather than life in certain situations. Regardless of the quantity or direction of desire, *xin*'s reflective and volitional capability allows people to pursue what is reasonable and what should be done.

Noticeable in Xunzi's notion of volitional *xin* is his claim that the exercise of the volition of *xin* must match what is reasonable (*li* 理). The desires are harmless, insofar as the exercise of the volition of *xin* corresponds to what is reasonable. Conversely, if the exercise of the volition of *xin* against the desires is not in accordance with what is reasonable, it can bring about a disastrous outcome. Because Xunzi describes the outcome of such judgment as order or chaos, it seems evident that accordance with what is reasonable refers to the proper application of a normative standard to a given situation. How, then, can the exercise of the volition of *xin* coincide with what is reasonable? Xunzi again returns to the intellectual aspect of *xin:* "Judging it possible and leading the way to it (*daozhi* 道之) is where the intelligence (*zhi* 知) must come into play" (85/22/64, Knoblock 22.5b). If *zhi* 知 can be taken as *zhi* 智 (knowledge, wisdom),[51] this implies that the reflective knowledge of whether the judgment is in accord with what is reasonable leads the way to desire. In this view, the volition of *xin* must be guided by *xin*'s correct judgment.

In the beginning of this discussion of the volitional aspect of *xin,* it was shown that the notion of the critical thinking of *xin* presupposes its volitional capability of *xin*. Now, conversely, it is evident that whether or not the exercise of the volition of *xin* is proper depends on *xin*'s judgment. Does this mean that it is possible for *xin*'s judgment to mislead the exercise of the volition of *xin?* If so, what causes *xin* to misjudge things? What is the remedy for *xin*'s misjudgment?

The Problem of the Blindness of *Xin* and *Xin*'s Capacities

Xunzi claims that "it is the common flaw of persons to be blinded (*bi* 蔽) by some small point of the truth and to shut [their *xin*] to the fundamental rationale of things (*dali* 大理)"[52] (78/21/1, Knoblock 21.1). As Knoblock points out, "the theme of 'blindness' and 'obsession' was conventional even in Confucius' time."[53] In the *Analects,* Confucius warns that "excessive fondness of a virtue" can becloud a person's judgments.[54] In the *Mencius,* as we have already seen, the sense organs can become beclouded because they are not capable of thinking.[55] Xunzi, while following the general idea of the notion of *bi* (being blinded, blindness, obscuration, obsession), employs the term more specifically in describing how *xin* can fail to judge a situation correctly:

> One can be blinded by desire or aversion, by the beginnings of things or their end, by what is remote or what is near, by broadness or shallowness, by antiquity or modernity. Since each of the myriad things evokes a different reaction, there is none that could not obsess (*bi*) *xin*. This is the common flaw of the operation of *xin* (*xinshuzhigonghuan* 心術之公患). (78/21/6–7, Knoblock 21.2)

As we have already noticed in our discussion of the embodied aspect of *xin*, notwithstanding its autonomous capability, *xin* also contains *xing*-like dispositional tendencies that can lead *xin*'s critical thinking astray.

Xin's confirmatory function with regard to empirical knowledge can also lead it to fixate on a partial point of view; for distinctions among things as the basis of empirical knowledge can obstruct *xin*'s ability to perform reflective thinking impartially. The result is that persons are obsessed by one aspect of things or one situation and cannot see things and the situation from a comprehensive, holistic perspective.[56] Xunzi specifically cites several philosophers who failed to see things in a comprehensive way:

> Mo Di was blinded by utility (*yong* 用) and was insensible to the value of good forms (*wen* 文). Song Xing was blinded by desire (*yu* 欲) and was insensible to satisfaction (*de* 得). Shen Dao was blinded by law (*fa* 法) and was insensible to worth (*xian* 賢). Shen Buhai was blinded by technique (*shi* 勢) and was insensible to knowledge (*zhi* 知). Hui Shi was blinded by propositions (*ci* 辭) and was insensible to realities (*shi* 實). Zhuang Zhou was blinded by *tian* 天 and was insensible to humans (*ren* 人). (79/21/21–22, Knoblock 21. 4)

According to Xunzi, while they are not totally wrong, they stick exclusively to "a single corner of *dao*" (79/21/24, Knoblock 21.4) and cannot see the whole picture.

How, then, can *xin* comprehend things without being blinded by some of their aspects? Xunzi holds that the sage who "knows the flaws of *xin*'s operation and perceives the misfortunes of blindness" overcomes this obstacle by "laying out all the myriad things and causing himself to exactly match how each settles on the suspended balance (*heng* 衡)" (79/21/29, Knoblock 21.5a). What is this balance? Xunzi replies that "it is *dao* 道" (79/21/29–30, Knoblock 21.5b). In other words, the gauge by which to measure a situation properly is *dao*. *Dao,* thus, is another name for what is reasonable (*li* 理)[57] or the fundamental rationale of things (*dali* 大理). However diverse the information or knowledge that is given through our sense organs and experience, Xunzi insists we can arrive at proper judgments with the knowledge of *dao*. The primary task for *xin* is, thus, to know *dao*. How does *xin* know *dao*? In answering this question, Xunzi does not bring up *xin*'s autonomous features or resort to some epistemological methodology. Instead, he says that *xin*'s capacity to know *dao* comes from its qualities of emptiness,[58] unity, and placidity:

> *Xin* never stops storing; nonetheless it possesses what is called emptiness (*xu* 虛). *Xin* never lacks plurality (*liang* 兩); nonetheless it possesses what is called unity (*yi* 一). *Xin* never stops moving;

> nonetheless it possesses what is called placidity (*jing* 靜). (80/21/35–36, Knoblock 21.5d)

As mentioned before, Xunzi borrows the notions of emptiness, unity, and placidity as the qualities or states of *xin* from Zhuangzi.[59] Also, Lee Yearley argues that Xunzi is much closer to Zhuangzi because he engages himself in the Zhuangzian problematic of "attachment" in "esoteric writings," where he emphasizes these qualities of *xin* as the conditions for comprehending *dao*.[60]

Now, let us see how Xunzi himself articulates the notions of emptiness, unity, and placidity as the capacities of *xin* that enables it to know *dao:*

> Persons from birth have awareness (*zhi* 知). Having awareness, there is memory (*zhi* 志). Memories are what is stored (*zang* 臧), yet *xin* has the property called emptiness. Not allowing what has previously been stored to interfere with what is being received in *xin* is called emptiness. *Xin* from birth has awareness. Having awareness, there is perception of difference. Perception of difference consists in awareness of two aspects of things at the same time. Awareness of two aspects of things at the same time entails duality; nonetheless, *xin* has the quality called unity. Not allowing the one thing to interfere with the other is called unity. When *xin* is asleep, it dreams. When it relaxes, it moves of its own accord. When it is employed in a task, it plans. Thus *xin* never stops moving; nonetheless it possesses the quality called placidity. Not allowing dreams and fantasies to bring disorder to awareness is called placidity. (80/21/36–39, Knoblock 21. 5d)

Even without an analysis of the Xunzian notions of emptiness, unity, and placidity, differences in the way Zhuangzi and Xunzi describe them are immediately apparent; while Zhuangzi portrays emptiness, unity, and placidity as achieved states of *xin,* based on the contrast between ordinary *xin* and achieved *xin,* Xunzi describes them as the functional qualities of *xin*. There cannot be found, in the *Xunzi,* any remarks about the mystical transformation of ordinary *xin* into achieved *xin*. In other words, Xunzi does not draw a sharp demarcation between ordinary *xin* and achieved *xin*.[61] Emptiness, unity, and placidity simply refer to the basic qualities or capacities that allow *xin* to know *dao;* if those qualities function properly, we can know *dao*. Put another way, these qualities are the epistemological foundations that allow *xin* to know *dao*.

It is important to examine each conception respectively. Humans are born with the ability to know things through sense perception. Knowledge gained through experience is accumulated and not forgotten. We call this memory. In spite of the vast amount of our accumulated knowledge and memories, we are able to receive new knowledge. This is because *xin* has the property called "emptiness." Knowing things through sense perception entails perceiving differences among things as well as in a thing at the same time. When we look at a tree in a garden, we can perceive a lot of things, such as the tree or its leaves, its trunk, its branches, at the same time. We recognize leaves as leaves, the trunk as the trunk, or the tree as the whole tree, without confusing the leaves with branches or a part of the tree with the tree as a whole. This capacity of *xin* to single out and attend to one thing or one aspect of a thing without confusion, while continually perceiving various things or different aspects of the thing, is called "unity." *Xin* is constantly working while dreaming, having reveries, or mulling things over for a certain plan or decision, and is also capable of a composed deliberation without being confused by an absurd fantasy or a jittery concern. This capacity of *xin* is called "placidity."

Compare these notions with those of Zhuangzi. First of all, Xunzi's notion of the emptiness of *xin* is explicated in terms of *xin*'s capacity to acquire new knowledge without being interrupted by the knowledge we already have, whereas Zhuangzi employs the conception as the achieved state of *xin,* in which *xin* is free of all desires and conventional normative judgments. To put it another way, while Zhuangzi stresses the literal emptiness of *xin,* Xunzi emphasizes the capacity of *xin* to constantly gain new knowledge. As for the notion of unity, while Zhuangzi underscores the transformative ability of *xin* to annihilate a barrier between a cognitive subject and a cognized object through the concentration of *xin,* Xunzi describes *xin*'s capacity to identify and concentrate on an object without being overwhelmed or distracted by constantly receiving multifarious impressions from different things or different aspects of the object. Finally, regarding the notion of placidity, Zhuangzi and Xunzi seem to share a similar view—that is, that *xin* has the ability to reflect things without distortion, like serene water.[62] However, there is a difference in emphasis between them; while Zhuangzi stresses the achieved state of *xin,* saying that "the sage's *xin* in placidity is the mirror of heaven and earth, the glass of the ten thousand things,"[63] Xunzi portrays "placidity" as a common faculty of *xin,* with which an ordinary person is able to distinguish between unreliable fantasies and deliberative thinking without much difficulty.

In short, Xunzi does not uncritically adopt the Zhuangzian notions of emptiness, unity, and placidity; rather, he appropriates them in a distinctively Xunzian way. Although he seems to share with Zhuangzi the problem of "attachment or blindness (*bi*) of *xin*" as an issue in gaining an impartial perspective, Xunzi's fundamental concern seems to lie not in the complete transformation of ordinary *xin* into achieved *xin,* but in the articulation of the capacities of *xin* to allow people to attain the knowledge of *dao.* In other words, Xunzi does not seem to employ the notions of emptiness, unity, and placidity for the purpose of describing a detached state of *xin* as an ultimate goal, but to articulate the preconditions for *xin* to attain and exercise the knowledge of *dao*. As David Nivison succinctly puts it, "this state of mind [*xin*] in Hsün Tzu [Xunzi] is a means to clear thinking and correct judgment, not a religious goal, not an end in itself [as in Zhuangzi]."[64]

Putting aside the question of how much Xunzi accepts a Zhuangzian stance in dealing with the problem of *bi* and the notion of the capacities of *xin* to be empty, unitary, and placid, Yearley also touches on a deeper issue concerning the character of *xin* in Xunzi's philosophy, that is, the contrast or the conflict between the notion of *xin* as "spectator" and as "director."[65] This issue is directly related to our discussion of Xunzi's notion of *xin*, because *xin* as director refers to its autonomous character, and *xin* as spectator refers to its emptiness, unity, and placidity. The problem is whether there is really any conflict between the autonomous *xin* and *xin* as the possessor of the qualities of emptiness, unity, and placidity. I have demonstrated that Xunzi's autonomous *xin* involves both intellectual and volitional aspects. As an intellectual faculty, *xin* performs critical thinking with regard to first-order desires. It presupposes *xin*'s volitional ability to be free from desires, emotions, and external circumstances. The exercise of the volition of *xin* hinges on whether *xin* properly comprehends a situation through critical reflection. To know whether *xin*'s judgment fits what is reasonable is to know *dao*. According to Xunzi, a person is born with the capacity to know *dao*. The problem is that a person is also born with *xin*, which can be easily biased or blinded by its attachment to a partial aspect of a thing due to various causes, such as desires, emotions, and the sense organs. Notwithstanding its problematic nature, *xin* can also know *dao*, because it has the qualities of emptiness, unity, and placidity. Xunzi puts it this way: "If you intend to seek *dao*, become empty and you can enter into it. If you intend to serve *dao*, attain oneness and you can exhaust it. If you intend to ponder *dao*, attain placidity and you can discern it" (80/21/39–40, Knoblock 21.5d). These qualities are inherent characteristics of *xin* that even an ordinary person possesses. Only difference between a sage and an ordinary person is that while the sage fully actualizes those qualities through vigilant discipline and incessant practice, the ordinary person does not. Now, the question may be asked again: Are these qualities inconsistent with the autonomous character of *xin?* It does not seem likely; emptiness, oneness, and placidity are the qualities that enable the organ of *xin* as the reflective thinking faculty to know *dao*. Put differently, these qualities are no other than the specific attributes of deliberative thinking that *xin* possesses as an autonomous faculty.

The reason *xin*'s judgment can mislead the exercise of its volition lies in *xin*'s tendency to fixate on a partial point of view or to be blinded by a partial aspect of a thing. The remedy for this propensity is, first, to recover or preserve *xin*'s capacity to be empty, unitary, and placid; then, *xin* is able to grasp *dao* and employ the knowledge of *dao* as the "balance" in comprehending and assessing things or a given situation. What, then, is *dao?* I hinted that Xunzi's *dao* refers to a holistic moral perspective with which a person can judge things in an undistorted fashion. What, then, specifically, comprises *dao,* and how can Xunzi claim that persons can know *dao* simply by keeping their *xin* empty, unitary, and placid? First, we need to recall that the sense of appropriateness (*yi* 義) is, according to Xunzi, an intuitive sense of morality inherent to *xin.* Although this intuitive quality lacks any concrete content, it allows persons to see what is desirable or what is reasonable in a given situation, and thus helps them promote humaneness and build a flourishing society. If the sense of appropriateness is the most fundamental ingredient of the notion of *dao,* it is not difficult to understand Xunzi's claim that, if *xin*'s basic qualities work properly, persons can gain the knowledge of *dao.* Given that *dao,* as a holistic Confucian moral vision, is based on the inherent intuitive sense of what is appropriate, it should be viewed not as some sort of "transcendental perspective" gained only through the mystical transformation of *xin,* but as a holistic viewpoint that is sensitive to particular situations as well as accessible through the proper exercise of the capacities of *xin.*

From the connection between *dao* and the sense of appropriateness, it can also be inferred that another important conception in Xunzi's philosophy, *li* 禮 (rituals, rite, etiquette, manner), is closely related to the notion of *dao.* As has frequently been pointed out, the sense of appropriateness and *li* are inseparable concepts for Xunzi. *Li* represents the formalized and embodied aspect of the sense of appropriateness. *Li* furnishes *dao* with specific and "formal prescriptions for proper behavior."[66] Accordingly, *li* can be deemed one of the core elements that embodies the spirit of *dao.* Thus, examining the character of *li* will provide a more concrete understanding of Xunzi's moral philosophy. It will also reveal how the autonomous *xin* builds a conventional and yet nonarbitrary morality.

Chapter 5

Li 禮 and Morality

Introduction

The examination of the autonomous character of *xin* in the *Xunzi* suggests that Xunzi's moral philosophy takes quite a different shape from other contemporary—particularly naturalistic—Chinese philosophies. Xunzi's autonomous *xin,* unlike that of Mencius, does not rely on natural, emotional dispositions in moral cultivation or ethical direction; it depends on its intellectual and volitional faculties in judging what is right. Those who have *xin* have an inherent capacity to know what is right or appropriate so long as *xin*'s disposition of being empty, unitary, and placid is not disrupted. This does not mean that Xunzi's notion of *xin* is similar to the Mencian notion of "genuine understanding (*liangzhi* 良知)" or "genuine ability (*liangneng* 良能)." Suppose a man who has never learned to swim falls into deep water by accident; if he possesses "genuine ability or understanding of how" to swim, he might escape drowning. Although there could be room for him to vastly improve his swimming skills, his "genuine ability" allows him to get out of the water instinctively. On the contrary, if he merely possesses a capacity to learn to swim, he is most likely going to drown without the aid of others. Unless he is taught how to swim, his potential ability to learn to swim does not help him avoid drowning. *Xin*'s capacity to know what is appropriate, or *dao,* for Xunzi, is like our capacity to learn to swim. The sense of appropriateness is a cognitive capacity that must await intellectual and volitional endeavors, without which persons will most likely lose their capacity to see *dao.*

This swimming analogy is readily applied to a comparison between Zhuangzi and Xunzi.[1] Zhuangzi might say that the drowning man can escape only if he stops making a distinction between himself and the water and assimilates himself to the flow of the water. Xunzi would reply that, although the man could employ the spontaneous flow of the water in swimming, he first has to learn to swim. As a first step, he has to know the appropriate way to swim. It could be to follow the natural flow of the water. However, there could be many different ways to follow the flow of the water, and he must choose what is the most appropriate way for him. Then, he must make a strenuous effort to learn that way of swimming. In short, even though the most appropriate way to swim turns out to be the most approximate imitation of the natural flow of the water, he must first exercise his intellect and volition in choosing and mastering that way of swimming. He is, after all, not water, and swimming is not a spontaneous activity, but a deliberate one he has to learn in order to cope with water.

What, then, is the most appropriate way to live a life and constitute a society? According to Xunzi, one of the most fundamental and concrete means of achieving a flourishing life and an orderly society lies in *li*. Our deliberative thinking leads us to adopt *li* as the best guide both to transform our disorder-prone, natural dispositions into well-channeled emotions and desires and to build a harmonious society. However, how can *li* claim such authority? Isn't it mere convention or a particular religious practice? According to Xunzi, although it is convention in the sense that *li* is established by the sage-kings and does not count on the sanction of *tian* for its legitimacy, it is not arbitrary. We encounter a similar contention in his theory of naming. Xunzi also holds that, although names are artifacts invented by the sages or the Later Kings, they are not merely conventional. Xunzi insists that those who bring confusion to the proper use of names should be punished severely. How can he claim such severe punishment for bringing disorder to the use of names while admitting the conventionality of names? An exploration of Xunzi's rationale in preserving the names established by the sage-kings and claiming, at the same time, the conventionality of names, would provide a valuable perspective for approaching his theory of *li*.

Conventional but Nonarbitrary Names

Xunzi begins his chapter "On the Proper Use of Names (*zhengming*正名)"[2] with the explication of the origins of various terminologies and names:

> The established names of the Later Kings (*houwang* 後王): They followed the Shang dynasty in the terminology of criminal law, the

> Zhou dynasty in the names of titles of rank and dignity, and the *Rituals* (*li* 禮) in the names of forms of culture. In applying miscellaneous names (*sanming* 散名) to the myriad things, they followed the established custom and general definitions of the central Xia states. For villages of distant regions that practice divergent customs, they relied on the standard terminology [of the Xia states] and enabled these villages to be put into communication. (82–83/22/1–2, Knoblock 22.1a)

Why does Xunzi ascribe the establishment of the standardization of names to the Later Kings, and not the Ancient Kings (*xianwang* 先王)?[3] If Xunzi's sole purpose were to solidify and legitimatize his conservative stance in his theory of names, the older the source of authority, the more authentic it would appear.[4]

The answer is to be found in the above quotation; Xunzi is very specific in explaining the source of the established names of the Later Kings: the terminology of criminal law is from the Shang dynasty, the names of titles of rank and dignity from the Zhou dynasty, the names of forms of culture from the *Rituals,* and miscellaneous names from the central Xia states. The terminology and names are not endowed by mystical, legendary sages from the remote past who are barely traceable. Knoblock confirms our observation: "Xunzi abandoned the way of Yao and Shun [Ancient Kings] because the high antiquity of their government did not allow us to know the specifics of their model. In contrast, Xunzi observes, we know in great detail the government of the Zhou dynasty."[5] Xunzi does not try to force an argument that the practices and norms of the Zhou dynasty should be identical with those of the Ancient Kings, Yao and Shun. Instead, he simply turns to the more available and practically suitable norms and institutions of the Zhou dynasty that those contemporary rulers should adopt. In the following statement, Xunzi goes even further and asserts that, given the chaotic situation, a true king would invent new names:

> Now since the sage kings are no more, the preservation of names is neglected, strange propositions have sprung up, names and their realities have become confused, and the boundary between right and wrong has become unclear. Even both officials charged with preserving the codes of law and the Confucians who recite their texts and enumerate their topics are also confused. Should a true king appear, he would certainly retain some old names but he would also have to invent new names. (83/22/10–12, Knoblock 22.2a)

The foregoing discussion anticipates Xunzi's explicit assertion that names have no essential properties that determine what it is to which they should be applied:

> Names have no intrinsic appropriateness (*mingwuguyi* 名無固宜). They are bound to something by agreement in order to name it. The agreement becomes fixed, the custom is established, and it is called "appropriate (*yi* 宜)." If a name differs from the agreed name, it is called "inappropriate (*buyi* 不宜)." Names have no intrinsic object (*gushi* 固實). They are bound to some reality by agreement in order to name the object. The object becomes fixed, the custom is established, and it is called the name of that object (*shiming* 實名). Names do have intrinsic goodness (*gushan* 固善); when names are straightforward, easy and not at odds with the things (*jingyierbufu* 徑易而不拂), we call them "good names (*shanming* 善名)." (83–84/22/25–27, Knoblock 22.2g)

Two important points are raised in the above paragraph; first, names are conventions agreed on by people, and second, although names are deemed conventional, there are "good names."

The "conventionalist" aspect in early Confucians's theories of naming has been given particular attention by scholars. Rendering *zhengming* as "the doctrine of rectification of names," Chad Hansen holds that the doctrine of *zhengming* in general, regardless of whether it is the Menican version or the Confucian and Xunzian version,[6] implies "conventionalism"[7]:

> The doctrine implies that actual name boundaries are determined by their actual use. The return-to-sage aspect of the doctrine entails that the names have been corrupted and changed by historical patterns of use and by gradual introductions of new distinctions. Furthermore, that political techniques on the part of the ruler can reestablish the boundaries set by the sages entails that the actual criteria of name use are changeable social practices.

Following this exposition of the general implication of the doctrine of *zhengming*, Hansen specifies the Xunzian version of conventionalism as a doctrine that holds that "the sage provides a single model which can coordinate and harmonize the way people make evaluative distinctions, cultivate attitudes, make choices, and act." It is conventionalist in that "implicitly, the argument seems to allow that any way of assigning names that was universally adopted (and met survival and effectiveness criteria) would be acceptable."[8]

A "performative" aspect may be added to the doctrine of *zhengming*. In analyzing Confucius' notion of *zhengming*, Hall and Ames elucidate its "performative" aspect in detail:

> In the immanental cosmos of Confucius, a correlative relationship obtains between idea and action, reason and experience, theory and

> praxis. Further, Confucian philosophy begins from an irreducibly interpersonal conception of the human beings in which self, society, and state are correlates determined through communication. Under these conditions, naming for Confucius cannot simply be a process of attaching appropriately corresponding labels to an already existing reality. The performative force of language entails the consequence that to interpret the world through language is to impel it towards a certain realization, to make it known in a certain way. And the extent to which one is able to influence the world is a function of the extent to which one can articulate his meaning, value, and purpose in such manner as to evoke deferential responses from others.[9]

The performative aspect seems to reinforce the conventionalist reading of the notion of *zhengming;* naming is not simply to establish a corresponding relation between a name and its object, but to impose an agent's intention on the world so as to "impel it toward a certain realization." However, Hansen carries his conventionalist reading of Xunzi's theory of naming to the point where he claims that it entails "traditionalism," with justification solely in "an appeal to argument from anarchy." Therefore, Xunzi, according to Hansen, does not claim that "the traditional values are rationally justified, but that messing with it [*sic*] will create chaos."[10] Yet can it really be said that Xunzi's "prescriptive conventionalism" has no rational justification other than an appeal to social order?

It is now necessary to address the second point, that "there are good names." Xunzi says that names which are straightforward (*jing* 徑), easy (*yi* 易), and not at odds with the things (*bufu* 不拂) are good. Notice that one of the criteria for a good name is whether or not it is at odds with the thing it names.[11] Why does a conservative traditionalist pay attention to the corresponding relation between a name and its object? If Xunzi's sole justification for naming is to preserve sociopolitical order, his criteria for good names do not seem to make much sense. At this point, it is significant to note that Xunzi asserts that those who "bring confusion to the correct use of names" are "to be punished as severely as the crimes of tampering with weights and measures" (83/22/13, Knoblock 22.1c). Measurement is invented to satisfy the human need to measure the world. However, while measurement is a human construction, it does not follow that measurement can be totally independent of the world. If it were based solely on human agreement and did not reflect the objective world at all, we could not possibly build bridges and houses and measurement would be useless. That is, although measurement is a human invention, it must not be "at odds with the world." This analogy of measurement may be taken even further. We know that there are different ways to measure the world, such as the system of metric units and the system of imperial units. If both systems are applicable to the world, the choice between these two systems would be a question of which one is more convenient or "easier" to use. If one of the systems is not applicable to the world, or is "at odds with the world," the question of which one is better would be obvious. Once we adopt a "good" system of measurement, "the tampering with weights and measures" must be punished severely, because this would bring not only confusion to the proper use of measurement but also catastrophic results, such as the collapse of bridges and buildings and distrust and miscommunication between the members of society.

Names, like measurement, while human inventions, are also not arbitrary or independent of the world, for there are good names, which are direct and easy, and also *not at odds with things*. Xunzi explains the purpose of "having names" as follows:

> They [wise persons] instituted names to refer to objects, making distinctions in order to make clear what is noble and what base and [making] separations in order to discriminate between things that are the same and those that are different. When the noble and base are clear and the same and the different are kept apart, conveying intentions is no longer frustrated through a failure to explain, and carrying out duties no longer suffers from being hampered and obstructed. This is the purpose of having names. (83/22/14–15, Knoblock 22.2b)

Recall that, for Xunzi, the sense of appropriateness (*yi* 義) is the capacity to see what is reasonable (*li* 理) and that what is reasonable is the hierarchical structure of society. Thus, the distinction between what is noble and what is base is as "natural" as the distinction between things that are the same and those that are different. In other words, names are instituted to satisfy "human and administrative needs"[12] and also to reflect the world as it is. Considering the "performative" aspect of Xunzi's theory of naming, names are also invented to reinforce the world as it ought to be on the basis of the world as it is.

The following passage offers evidence to suggest that Xunzi thinks of names as "nonarbitrary" and the reason for this:

> What is the basis of deeming something the same or different? I say that it is based on the sense organs given us by nature. As a general rule, whenever things belong to the same category of being (*tonglei* 同類) or have the same defining characteristics (*tongqing* 同情), the representation of them presented by the senses is the same. Thus, when put side by side and compared, they resemble each other and are fully interchangeable. That is why they are given a general conventional name and used to define each other. (83/22/15–17, Knoblock 22.2c)

The above passage was discussed earlier with regard to Xunzi's epistemology. At that time, it was examined out of context for the purpose of investigating the manner in which Xunzi thinks knowledge is acquired. Now it is clear that Xunzi regards his theory of naming to be closely related to the epistemological structure of how we perceive the world. For Xunzi, although names are conventional artifacts created to refer to objects, as we do not perceive the world in an idiosyncratic, human way, but recognize things according to "natural categories (*lei* 類)" to which they belong, or "natural characteristics (*qing* 情)" that they possess, names must also reflect the world appropriately.

Thus far, Xunzi's theory of naming has exhibited two aspects. On the one hand, when he ascribes established names to the Later Kings and claims the conventionalist aspect of names, he appears to be a flexible, pragmatic thinker. On the other hand, when he advocates conformity to standardized language and harsh punishment for bringing confusion to the proper use of names, he appears unyielding and conservative. These dual aspects of Xunzi can be explained as follows: although Xunzi holds a "conventionalist" position regarding the theory of naming, in his denial of the "essential" relationship between a name and its object, he does not insist that names can be arbitrarily invented or instituted without taking into consideration their applicability to the world. Rather, Xunzi seems to believe that even in order for the language to exert a "performative" function properly, it first has to give due respect to the world as it is; otherwise, language would be ineffectual and disastrous to sociopolitical order, which is not just a human invention, but also a part of the cosmic order. However, since names themselves have no intrinsic appropriateness, if we have lost the names instituted by the Ancient Kings or find a better alternative to meet the criteria for good names, we could invent new names or adopt a better alternative. Language, for Xunzi, is, after all, a pragmatic instrument to "convey our intentions" and to "carry out our duties."

Li

The notion of *li* encompasses such a wide range of implication that it is almost impossible to find a single matching word in English. Among a long list of translations of *li*, a particularly accurate one is given by Peter A. Boodberg: "Propriety, ritual (religious and social), cult and culture, worships, ceremony and ceremonial, etiquette, decorum, decency and refinement, urbanity, courtesy, rules of proper social usages or conduct, customary rules of living, polite traditional deportment, good manners, social order, *convenance, bienséance, Sittlichkeit,* formality, good form."[13] Cua nicely captures the implication of *li* in a more succinct manner: "In general, the notion of *li* refers to a normative domain consisting of rites, ceremonies, decorum, courtesy, and civility, which may conveniently be labeled 'the domain of propriety.'"[14]

On the surface, it might seem that *li* as "the domain of propriety" has nothing to do with language. However, if the fundamental idea underlying Xunzi's theory of language, namely *zhengming*, is compared with his notion of *li*, an unexpected similarity becomes evident between them: Xunzi bases both theories on the distinction between those things that are the same and those that are different and the discrimination between what is noble and what is base. Put otherwise, "making distinctions (*fen* 分)" is, for Xunzi, the primary function of both language and *li*. In addition, Xunzi emphasizes the "performative" aspect of language. Naming things not only reflects the world as it is, but serves to shape the world as it should be. This "perfomative" aspect is even more conspicuous in the theory of *li*. The most fundamental assumption in the theory is that *li* can bring about an orderly society. By making social distinctions explicit and internalized by the members of society, *li* can make society harmonious and without conflict.[15]

Based on these similarities, we can anticipate how Xunzi establishes his theory of *li* as a moral theory that is not merely conventional; the sage-kings create *li* to order society, and yet, since *li* is inseparable from the sense of appropriateness, which is directly connected to what is reasonable, it is neither arbitrary nor unreasonable. Keeping these dual aspects of *li* in mind, I examine more closely in the next section the characteristics of the Xunzian notion of *li*.

The Origin of *Li*

Just as chaotic historical circumstances compel Xunzi to clarify the theory of *zhengming*, his theory of *li* is also a product of the historical situation in which the notion of *li* becomes "opaque" in the sense that not only other philosophical schools such as the Mohists, the Daoists, and the Legalists, but also rival Confucian schools, represented by the Mencian school, compete for an appropriate evaluation and understanding of *li*.[16] The Mohists hold that *li* is a useless, ornamental activity that requires extravagant expenditure. The Daoists argue that *li* is something against human natural dispositions and serves only as an obstacle to achieving spontaneity. The Legalists say that *li* is useful only when it amounts to law. Mencius asserts that *li* comes from natural human emotional tendencies. Against this background, Xunzi asserts that *li* is an artifact established by the sage-kings to properly curb and nurture destructive natural desires, enabling the members of society to peacefully satisfy their desires:

> How did *li* arise? I say that persons are born with desires which, if not satisfied, cannot but lead persons to seek to satisfy them. If in seeking to satisfy their desires persons observe no measure and apportion things without limits (*wuduliangfenjie* 無度量分界), then it would be impossible for them not to contend over the means to satisfy their desires. The Ancient Kings (*xianwang* 先王) abhorred such disorder; so they established *li* and what is appropriate (禮義) in order to apportion things (*fenzhi* 分之), to nurture the desires of persons (*yangrenzhiyu* 養人之欲), and to supply the means for their satisfaction (*geirenzhiqiu* 給人之求). They saw to it that the desires did not overextend the means for their satisfaction and material goods (*wu* 物) were not exhausted by the desires. In this way the two of them, desires and goods, sustained each other over the course of time. This is the origin of *li*. (70/19/1–3, Knoblock 19.1a)

While ascribing the need for inventing new names simply to the chaotic sociopolitical situation, Xunzi, in discussing the origin of *li*, explores a more fundamental source of social disorder: human desires. As we have observed previously, Xunzi believes that human spontaneous dispositions are so unreliable that, without due control or cultivation, they tend to exert a bad influence on the individual agent's critical thinking and also disrupt the fundamental soundness of the whole society. It is remarkable that Xunzi gives one of his most vivid descriptions of the destructive human dispositional tendencies in explaining the origin of *li*. The Ancient Kings, facing a chaotic social situation resulting from unbridled desires seeking unlimited satisfaction, established not laws or other coercive disciplinary measures, but *li* and morality "to apportion things, to nurture the desires of persons, and to supply the means for their satisfaction." *Li* is, thus, not the outcome of spontaneous moral dispositions, but an artificial construction to cope with those spontaneous dispositions. How can *li* be a solution to disorder-prone natural dispositions? What is the underlying idea in promoting the notion of *li* as something that guides our action and organizes our society? First, I examine Xunzi's assertion that one of the major functions of *li* is to "nurture the desires of persons." When it is clear how *li* can nurture the desires, it will be possible to answer the first question.

The Functions of *Li*

Xunzi specifically ascribes "nurturing the desires of persons" to the function of *li*. How can *li* nurture human desires? Xunzi gives a very concrete description of the activities of "nurturing":

> The meat of pastured and grain-fed animals, rice and millet, blends and combinations of the five flavors, are what nurture the mouth. The fragrances of peppercorns and orchids, aromas and bouquets, are what nurture the nose . . . Spacious rooms, secluded chambers, mats of plaited rushes, couches and bed mats, armrests and cushions, are what nurture the body. Thus, *li* is what nurtures. (70/19/3–5, Knoblock 19.1b)

Questions may arise regarding two points: First, how does the above description of nurturing the sense organs lead to the conclusion that "*li* is what nurtures," and, second, how can Xunzi shift the topic from "nurturing the desires of persons" to that of nurturing the sense organs without any explanation? The latter question seems not to require much explanation. The sense organs, emotions, and desires are all included in Xunzi's notion of *xing,* which denotes passively responsive human faculties. Therefore, the sense organs, emotions, and desires, for Xunzi, are likely to be closely interrelated notions. A person desires to satisfy his or her sensory appetites: the eyes desire to see beautiful things, the mouth desires to eat delicious food, the body desires comfort, and so on. In the same way, a person desires to express his or her emotional feelings. These are all given characteristics of our natural dispositional tendencies. *Li* is a set of deliberately devised "formal prescriptions" that restrain and refine those natural dispositions. Thus, it seems natural that Xunzi has no difficulty shifting the discussion of nurturing (*yang* 養) from "nurturing the desires of persons" to "nurturing the sense organs."

How, then, is *li* related to nurturing the sense organs? First, we need to be aware that this material manner of nurturing the sense organs aims to satisfy the appetites of these organs. In other words, by "nurturing," Xunzi means satisfying basic material needs. How can *li* be said to satisfy basic material needs? The answer depends on Xunzi's discussion of the origin of *li*. In mentioning how *li* can bring about social order, Xunzi refers to "apportioning things (*fenzhi* 分之)" as one of the major functions of *li*. "Apportioning things" means not only distinguishing between things that are the same and those that are different, but also demarcating the higher, noble social class from the lower, base one.[17] One of the most significant functions of *li* is, thus, to serve as the standard for making explicit distinctions between the members of different social classes.

However, it is important to remember that *li* is not restricted to a set of formal standards for making distinctions within the social hierarchy. *Li* is also an educational system through which to channel each person's desires toward goals appropriate to his or her station. Thus, Xunzi can say that *li* and morality can ensure that "the desires do not overextend the means for their satisfaction and material goods are not exhausted by the desires." Henry Rosemont,

Jr., gives a good analysis of how *li* can serve to direct one's desires: "By establishing goals for each social level, it is insured that not everyone will desire the same things at the same time, increasing the probability that everyone will realize a certain percentage of his goals."[18]

In sum, the reason *li* can be said to nurture the desires of persons or satisfy basic material needs is because material resources can be peacefully redistributed by its dual functions: *li* functions, first, as the standard for making the social hierarchical system clear, and second, as an educational system that renders the members of the society able to pursue desires appropriate to their social levels. This prompts another question: How does *li* channel our desires? Extending the scope of this question, Xunzi may be asked how *li* can be supposed to direct our disorder-prone, natural dispositions in general. The remarkable passage in which Xunzi explicates the sacrificial rite in terms of emotional expressions gives us a glimpse of how he sees *li* as being able to direct natural dispositions:

> The sacrificial rite originates in the emotions stirred by remembrance and recollection of the dead and by thinking of and longing for the departed. There inevitably are occasions in everyone's life when he is seized by an unexpected change of mood, when feelings of disquietude and melancholy cause him to sigh involuntarily or to feel that his breath is short from deep emotion. Thus, even in the midst of enjoying himself with congenial company, the loyal minister and the filial son are sometimes profoundly moving. If they are repressed, the emotions stirred by remembrance of the dead with such matters will seem lacking and incomplete. Thus, the Ancient Kings established proper forms (*wen* 文) to be observed on occasions so that persons could carry out what is appropriate such as paying honor to those deserving honor and showing affection to those whom they cherished (*zunzunqinqinzhiyi* 尊尊親親之義). (75/19/117–120, Knoblock 19.11)

Noteworthy in this passage is that Xunzi advocates *li* not because it can regulate natural emotions by suppressing and denying them, but because it can refine and give direction to those emotions. Following is an example of the illustrations Xunzi gives to explain how the sacrificial rite can channel emotions: "The unhemmed garment of the mourner, his clothes of sackcloth and his bamboo staff, the lean-to hut where he lives, the gruel he eats, his brushwood mat, and his clod of earth for a pillow" are all considered "the proper forms expressive of his changed feelings of grief and pain" (75–76/19/123–124, Knoblock 19.11). In short, *li* guides natural dispositions not as a suppressive, formal, mechanistic code of behavior, but as an aesthetically refined behavior prescription conducive to expressing emotions and meeting desires. It is, thus, no wonder that Xunzi esteems *li* as the highest human cultural achievement (*wei* 偽), through which society attains social harmony and each member of society fulfills his or her material needs and spiritual well-being.

Li as a Practice

We have seen that Xunzi considers *li* not only a means for the preservation and welfare of society, but also an educational system intended to refine and give direction to natural dispositions. However, given that *li* as an educational system reinforces *li* as a methodical device for the maximization of social welfare, should the Xunzian notion of *li* be viewed purely as an "instrumentalist" or a "functionalist" conception? In other words, does Xunzi adopt *li* simply as a kind of "utilitarian" or "consequentialist" means to promote the maximization of social welfare?

Let us return to the passage where Xunzi argues that "the sacrificial rite originates in the emotions." At the end of this paragraph, it is evident that one does what is appropriate (*yi* 義), such as "paying honor to those who deserve honor and showing affection to those whom one cherishes," by virtue of the emotional expressions engendered by the sacrificial rite. In this view, *li* is almost inseparable from Confucian moral virtues, in that virtuous emotions cannot be expressed without proper forms given by *li*. On the surface, this might appear similar to the Mencian view of *li* because Mencius also advocates *li* as the expression of morality. However, closer investigation readily reveals the difference between Xunzi's notion of *li* and that of Mencius. For Mencius, as shown in the expression, "the heart of courtesy and modesty (*cirangzhixin* 辭讓之心) is the germ of *li* (*lizhiduan* 禮之端)," *li* is rooted in our natural emotional dispositions.[19] In contrast, for Xunzi, *li* is not the direct outcome of natural emotional dispositions, but the expressive forms by which one gives vent to natural emotions and transforms them into virtuous emotions.

While this argument, again, seems to lead to the instrumental function of *li* in Xunzi, it does not. Without *li*, there are, for Xunzi, no virtues at all. In other words, without the appropriate standards and forms provided by *li*, there is no way to develop virtuous character. Xunzi is very explicit about this:

> *Li* is the highest achievement of the way (*dao*) of human kind. Therefore, those who do not model after (*fa* 法) *li* and are not satisfied with *li* are called people who lack any method or standard (*fang* 方). (72/19/34, Knoblock 19.2d)

Following this statement, Xunzi depicts how the level of sagehood is achieved:

> Those who model themselves after *li* and find satisfaction in *li* are said to be scholars (*shih* 士) who have method and standards. Those who dwell in *li* and can ponder it well (*sisuo* 思索) are said to know how to think (*lu* 慮). Those who dwell in *li* and do not change their way are said to be steadfast. One who, being able to think and to stay steadfast, adds to them a fondness for *li*—this is to be a sage. (72/19/34–36, Knoblock 19.2d)

At first, persons are advised to adopt *li* as a method or standard by which to develop their moral characters and control their desires appropriate to their social stations. However, if they are able to ponder *li,* to carry on *li*-practices steadfastly, and finally to be fond of *li,* they arrive at the highest achieved level of personality, that of a sage. Therefore, *li* is no longer merely a standard or method for the sage. A sage is someone who no longer sees *li* simply as a means to develop his moral character; he understands the profound significance of *li* as "the highest achievement of the way of human kind," abides by *li*-prescriptions without fail, and, most important, has a fondness for *li* itself.

It is important to note that, in this description of sagehood, a sage has dual perspectives. On the one hand, he comprehends the significance of *li* from the point of view of a spectator. On the other, because he thoroughly internalizes *li*-practices, he is completely at home with and enjoys *li.* This is a level only a committed practitioner, not a spectator, can reach. One of the reasons the notion of *li* is so elusive to theoretical investigation is that it is not only multidimensional, but also "practical" rather than "theoretical." As Robert Eno has pointed out, *li* is closer to Michael Polanyi's notion of "skill" and Alasdair MacIntyre's notion of "practice" than to abstract moral maxims or principles.[20] If we borrow MacIntyre's notion of "practice" in explaining the intrinsic value of *li,* it can be said that *li* is not just a means to achieve external goods such as social order, but a "practice" through which "goods internal to that form of activity are realized."[21]

In summary, *li* is first conceived as a means to channel human desires and achieve social order. Once people are deeply involved in *li*-activities, they internalize *li* as a "practice" that generates goods internal to *li*-activities. Thus, *li* is not merely an instrumental method, but a virtue-generating practice that entails a deep emotional involvement with *li* and an aesthetic appreciation of it: "All *li* begin with coarseness, are brought to fulfillment in elegant form (*wen* 文), and end with pleasure and beauty. *Li* reaches its highest perfection when both emotion (*qing* 情) and form are fully realized" (71/19/25–26, Knoblock 19.2c).

An "Objective" Aspect in the Notion of *Li*

In this section, I return to the comparison between language and *li* in Xunzi's thought to further articulate the justification of *li* as a moral system. I have hinted that, given the "performative" and distinction-making functions of both language and *li* in Xunzi's thought, the reason *li* is not merely conventional might appear similar to the reason language is both conventional and not arbitrary; that is, although *li* is created by the sage-kings, the prerequisite for its "performative" function to impel the world to a certain realization is its reflection of the order of the world. First, that what is appropriate (*yi* 義) for Xunzi turns out to be the hierarchical division of society. As already stated, Xunzi considers the distinction between what is noble and what is base to be as "natural" as the distinction between things that are the same and those that are different. The difference between the social distinction and the natural distinction is that, while the latter needs no human intervention or endeavor, the former requires active human work. Put simply, the social distinction is human construction based on natural order. Therefore, the "naturalness" of the social distinction is not just given, but achieved by human effort.

Second, Xunzi connects *li* with heaven and earth, natural phenomena and natural human dispositions:

> Through *li*, heaven and earth are conjoined, the sun and moon shine brightly, the four seasons observe their natural precedence, the stars and planets move in ranks, the river and streams flow, and the myriad things prosper. Through *li,* love and hate are tempered, and joy and anger made to fit the occasion. (71/19/26–27, Knoblock 19.2c)

How can *li* be said to join in harmony with heaven and earth, or conduce natural phenomena to order and prosperity? One answer could be that *li*'s function in channeling a person's desire so that material resources are not exhausted can preserve natural order.[22] However, a more fundamental answer lies in Xunzi's belief that, as people follow and internalize *li*—which not only reflects cosmic order, but propels it toward a certain realization—it can achieve a human society where its harmony forms a trinity with the harmony of heaven and earth. What is crucial in this belief is that *li* does not go against the natural order.[23] If *li,* as a human construction, serves only to maximize social welfare and is deemed merely a conventional, social contract that does not take into consideration natural order, Xunzi could not possibly endorse it.

Finally, consider how Xunzi criticizes other schools, particularly the Legalists. He asserts that "the reasonableness of *li* (*lizhili* 禮之理) is so genuinely great that when people who create statues and regulations on their authority and advance despised and backward theories enter the domain of *li*, they are brought to ruin" (71/19/31, Knoblock 19.2d).[24] Xunzi does not criticize the Legalists on the ground that they ignore that *li* is created by the sage-kings. Instead, he contends that "they are brought to ruin" because the statutes and regulations they create lack the reasonableness of *li* and depend only on their arbitrary authority. After attacking various philosophical groups through the notion of the reasonableness of *li,* Xunzi explicates the reasonableness and genuineness of *li* in the following way:

> Thus, if the blackened marking line is properly stretched, then there can be no doubt about crooked and straight; if the scales are properly hung, there can be no doubt about heavy and light; if the compass and square are properly adjusted, there can be no doubt about square and round. So too, if the examplary person is thoroughly acquainted with *li,* then he cannot be fooled by fraud and pretense. (71/19/32–33, Knoblock 19.2d)

As was pointed out in the analogy of measurement in the earlier discussion of the conventionality and nonarbitrariness of language, the fact that *li* is invented by the sage-kings does not entail that it is unreasonable, arbitrary, and totally independent of the world. Because *li* has reasonableness and applicability in the same way as a compass and square, someone who is well-versed in *li* is able to see what is genuine and reasonable.

At this juncture, it seems unavoidable to mention a strong "realist" or "objectivist" reading of Xunzi's theory of *li* or ethicopolitical theory in general.[25] This reading holds that, while Xunzi admits the conventionality of *li* and language, his belief that people can properly complete the trinity with heaven and earth is based on his understanding of *li* and *dao* as a unique and unalterable system of morality and "the uniquely optimal Way for structuring a society."[26] Let us cite the following passages translated by Watson that are supposed to lend support to this reading:[27]

> There are not two Ways in the world (*tianxiawuerdao* 天下無二道); the sage is never of two minds (*shengrenwuliangxin* 聖人無兩心). (78/21/1, Knoblock 21.1, Watson 121)
>
> When *li* is properly established and brought to peak of perfection (*ji* 極), no one in the world can add to or detract from them. (71/19/28–29, Knoblock 19.2c, Watson 94)
>
> Music (*leyezhe* 樂也者) embodies an unchanging harmony (*huozhilebukebianzheye* 和之不可變者也), while *li* represents unalterable reason (*lizhilibukeyizheye* 理之不可易者也). (77/20/33, Knoblock 20.3, Watson 117)

> The Way is the proper standard for past and present (*gujinzhizhengquanye* 古今之正權也). (86/22/74, Knoblock 22.6b, Watson 153)

Before examining the above passages, it would be illuminating to first look at the following passage: "*Dao* itself is constant in its form yet completely changeable (*tichangerjinbian* 體常而盡變)" (79/21/24–25, Knoblock 21.4). This statement in the chapter "Dispelling Blindness" appears in the context of criticizing various philosophical schools' doctrines for their lack of holistic vision. For Xunzi, *dao* is not just a particular point of view, is a metaperspective by which to "treat things in all their combinations as things" (80/21/52, Knoblock 21.6b). Therefore, the underlying notion of *dao* as a holistic perspective cannot be alterable. However, since the holistic perspective, for Xunzi, is not an abstract, theoretical point of view from which all particulars can be deduced, but is rather an embodied vision gained through the experience of every possible particular events and self-cultivation, which renders such experience impartial and unprejudiced, *dao* must be capable of embracing all changes.

Since *dao* is a holistic perspective that does not lose sight of particulars, a "realist" or "objectivist" reading of the above statements seems less plausible. The notion of a holistic perspective hinges not on an abstract, fixed, principle such as the utilitarian one found in the expression of "the uniquely optimal Way for constructing a society," but on a concrete vision open to ever-changing circumstances and particulars without being blinded to a partial aspect of the world. From this perspective, it would not be necessary to employ a strong "realist" reading to understand the above passages related to the notion of *dao*. The world does not have two *daos,* because the notion of holistic vision itself presupposes all-encompassing comprehensiveness. *Dao,* as a holistic vision from antiquity to present, has been the only perspective from which to weigh things properly. That is, while *dao* in its form is deemed "unique" because it is an all-encompassing, holistic perspective, *dao* in its concrete content cannot be understood as "the first principle," because it is based, not on a fixed, abstract principle, but on a concrete vision flexible to all changing circumstances.

The more problematic passages seem to be those concerning the notion of *li*. The crucial question is whether those passages imply that *li* is unrevisable due to its "objective" character. Recall, again, the analogy of measurement. If we adopt the system of imperial units in measurement and it works well, there would be no need to "add to or detract from" it. However, it does not follow that we should not or must not replace it with a system of metric units if warranted by a change in circumstances. Similarly, given that *li* is the concrete embodiment of *dao* that must encompass all changes, to argue that *li* is unalterable and unrevisable is unpersuasive. What is unalterable is only that *li* reflects the definitional, tautological aspect of what is reasonable (*li* 理); that is, what is reasonable is not arbitrary. As "*dao* is constant in its form yet completely changeable," what is reasonable is unalterable in its form, but completely changeable in its application to a particular given situation. Granted, the sage-kings invented *li* according to the order of the world, but the "objectivity" gained from the knowledge of *li,* in its nature as the concrete embodiment of *dao,* is not that which claims the unchanging, absolute standard independently of human affairs. Rather, it is that which does justice to every particular, changing circumstance without being biased by a particular thing or a partial aspect of the world.

Li and the Autonomy of *Xin*

I have argued that Xunzi's notion of autonomy of *xin* leads him to adopt *li* as moral guidance for cultivating our moral character and constructing a harmonious society. How could Xunzi, while emphasizing the autonomy of *xin* in his philosophical anthropology, advise persons to follow and internalize customary *li* rather than to exercise their own autonomous, intellectual and volitional capacities? This question may raise another question: As long as Xunzi can be said to seek morality, not from an internal source, but from without, is Xunzi not much closer to the Legalists than the Confucians? The Legalists seek an "objective," nonarbitrary standard to establish social order, in the same way Xunzi finds in *li* the best available means to maximize social welfare. Is it thus no coincidence that Han Fei, the most famous Legalist theorist, and Li Si, the most famous Legalist politician, were Xunzi's disciples? Implicit in these questions is the following assumption: without assuming inner moral tendencies, there remains only one alternative for a philosophically defensible way of life in ancient Chinese philosophy, the Daoist way, which finds an ethical direction in the spontaneous way of nature. Since Xunzi does not adopt either way, there is no alternative for him but to appeal to external, authoritarian norm in his ethicopolitical philosophy.

In light of the above, the question of whether Xunzi is closer to the Legalists than the Confucians should be answered by examining the way in which Xunzi grounds his moral theory. This examination will, in turn, lead us to see more clearly how Xunzi's notion of the autonomy of *xin* can be related to his notion of *li.* First, I introduce the main tenet of Legalism and analyze the comparison between Xunzi and Han Fei made by Lao Siguang. This will lay the groundwork for an examination of Xunzi's moral theory in terms of the relation between Xunzi's moral theory and his notion of *xin*.

Legalism and Xunzi

Differing from other philosophical traditions, particularly Confucianism, Legalist thought finds its ideal model, not in legendary sage-kings, but in practical statesmen such as Guan Zhong 管仲 (B.C. 700) and Shang Yang 商鞅 (d. 338 B.C.E).[28] These statesmen share a primary concern not with the moral cultivation of rulers as the political norm, but with devising a practical political means to establish sociopolitical order. Legalist philosophy was developed throughout the politically turbulent period, and the notions of *fa* 法 (law, model, standard, regulation) [29] and *shu* 術 (methods, policies, tact, arts of governing) emerged as the central Legalist conceptions. The following statement by Han Fei 韓非 (d. 233 B.C.E), a great synthesizer of Legalist thought, reveals the core idea of Legalism:

> Now Shen Pu-hai 申不害 speaks of method (*shu*) but Lord Shang [Shang Yang] deals in laws (*fa*). Method is bestowing office suiting assignments to qualifications, making responsible for the object as laid down by the name, holding fast to the Handles which deal death or life, and testing the abilities of all the ministers. These are in the hands of the ruler. Law is having the statutes publicly available in the government offices, punishments which the people know for certain will be applied, rewards given consistently for punctiliousness in the law, and punishments imposed consistently on violators of the decrees. These are what the subjects take as their exemplars. Without method for the ruler there are abuses up above, without law for the subject there is disorder down below. Neither is dispensable, both are tools for emperor or king.[30]

Most noticeable in Han Fei's exposition of *fa* and *shu* is that these notions appear to have no connection to the moral qualities of the agents involved, either as the object of *fa* and *shu* or as the subject who employs method and institutes laws and regulations. They seem to serve only to enhance the ruler's political authority or preserve political order. Thus, the following comparison between Legalism and Confucianism made by Wing-Tsit Chan is not just a modern scholar's view, but is widely shared by traditional Confucian scholars and other contemporary scholars:

> The Confucianists were dedicated to the cultivation of virtue, the development of individual personality, government for the people, social harmony, and the use of moral principles, moral examples, and moral persuasion. On the contrary, the Legalists were primarily inter-

ested in the accumulation of power, the subjugation of the individual to the state, uniformity of thought and the use of force.[31]

If this is the case, how, then, can Xunzi be compared to the Legalists? Discussing Xunzi's influence on Han Fei, Lao Siguang mentions three points.[32] First, Han Fei, accepting Xunzi's assertion that persons can be transformed by teachers and models (*shifa* 師法), emphasizes that governing people must rely on "re-forming (*gaizao* 改造)"[33] them by means such as punishment and reward, so that they will obey the commands of a ruler voluntarily. Second, Lao Siguang maintains that Han Fei shares Xunzi's view that human *xing* is bad. This doctrine could provide justification for Han Fei's authoritarian political theory, which asserts that people are uncontrollable without severe penal laws and reward. The following passage vividly shows how extreme Han Fei's position is regarding human *xing:*

> Besides, parents in relation to children, when males are born, congratulate each other, and, females are born, lessen the care of them. Equally coming out from the bosoms and lapels of the parents, why should boys receive congratulations while girls are ill-treated? Because parents consider their future conveniences and calculate their permanent benefits. Thus, even parents in relation to children use the calculating mind in treating them, how much more should those who have no affection of parent and child?[34]

Finally, and most significantly, according to Lao Siguang, Xunzi's moral philosophy itself has an element that entails Han Fei's authoritarianism: "In Xunzi's thought, his moral theory can be said to be a failure. Since he ascribes the source of value neither to internal *xin,* nor to external *tian,* he cannot but turn to authoritarianism."[35]

Without close scrutiny, the first two points that Han Fei is said to share with Xunzi might appear to be correct. However, on further examination, there appears a subtle, but significant, difference between the two, and that this difference is also crucial in examining the validity of the third claim, that Xunzi's ethical theory, which is based neither on internal *xin* nor external *tian*/nature, cannot escape having an authoritarian inclination. The difference lies in Xunzi's notion of *xin.* Lao Siguang overlooks that the most important conception in Xunzi's philosophical psychology is not the notion of *xing,* but that of *xin,* and that the central feature of the notion of *xin* is its faculty of self-governance, which bases its cognitive and volitional functions on the sense of appropriateness (*yi* 義) inherent in *xin.* Given the notion of the autonomy of *xin,* it seems clear that what Xunzi advocates is not the imposing "reformation (*gaizao* 改造) of people" through manipulative or coercive means, but the voluntary "transformation of their own natural tendencies (*huaxing* 化性)" by virtue of the exercise of the autonomous faculties of *xin.* Moreover, as I have already argued, Xunzi's assertion that human *xing* is bad should not be interpreted literally; it means, rather, that following our natural tendencies without being guided and transformed by *xin* can lead to disastrous results. In other words, when Xunzi claims that human *xing* is bad, he does not intend to say that humans are essentially and incorrigibly bad, but that, without the active employment of the autonomous faculties of *xin,* we have a tendency to be selfish in a way that is detrimental to the building of a harmonious society. Only this interpretation of his doctrine of the badness of *xing* seems to allow Xunzi to claim without contradiction that human *xing* is transformable. In spite of its destructive tendency, *xing* is transformable and, without it, there would be no base on which *xin* could exercise deliberative activity (*wei* 偽): "If there were no human *xing,* there would be nothing for deliberative activity to work upon, and if there were no deliberative activity, then human *xing* would have no way to refine itself" (73/19/76, Knoblock 19.6). In light of the foregoing analysis of the relation between Xunzi's notions of *xing* and *xin,* it seems highly unlikely that Xunzi approves of Han Fei's pessimistic view of human nature.

Finally, it is necessary to examine Lao Siguang's criticism that Xunzi fails to establish his moral theory on a philosophically defensible ground and therefore has to appeal to authoritarianism. This criticism is based on the assumption that, because Xunzi rejects both naturalistic sources of moral value—natural emotional dispositions (*xing*) and the spontaneous way of nature (*tian* or *ziran* 自然)—there is nothing for him to do but appeal to authoritarianism. As already mentioned, the ultimate basis on which the autonomous *xin* can exercise its critical thinking, according to Xunzi, is the sense of appropriateness *xin* already possesses. Therefore, it can be said that Xunzi also bases his ethical theory on *xin*'s internal property, which is connected to *tian.* What separates Xunzi from naturalists is not that he appeals to completely arbitrary external standards in establishing his moral theory; he does no such thing. Rather, Xunzi makes it clear that, because the sense of appropriateness as the source of morality is nothing more than an intuitive awareness, it is tenuous and easily overwhelmed by destructive natural dispositions without intellectual and volitional endeavor. By contrast, Zhuangzi and Mencius, preoccupied with the problem of the source of value, overemphasize the "naturalness" of the source of values and do not take seriously the importance of the deliberative effort of *xin* and the difference between its natural dispositions and its intellectual and volitional faculties. Because Lao Siguang also takes the naturalistic philosophers' viewpoint as his criterion in judging Xunzi, he fails to see that Xunzi's philosophical project aims to challenge such naturalistic tendencies of contemporary philosophers. Thus, Xunzi, instead of emphasizing the source of value, stresses deliberative activity as the focal point of his ethical theory. In short, Xunzi not only establishes his moral theory on the solid ground of the autonomy of *xin* and of the sense of appropriateness, he also offers a sound criticism of naturalistic philosophy.

Apart from the differences between Xunzi and Han Fei, another crucial difference between Xunzi and the Legalists is the distinction between the notion of *li* and the notions of *fa* and *shu*. At first glance, Xunzi and the Legalists seem to share the same motive in emphasizing *li*, *fa*, and *shu*. The appeal to the individual's moral sentiments or to individualistic retreat from society for the sake of following the spontaneous way of nature can no longer be considered a plausible, realistic solution to the cruel realities of the late Warring States period. Thus, Xunzi and the Legalists both look for a more secure, objective base on which to establish sociopolitical order. While Xunzi proposes *li*, the Legalists suggest *fa* and *shu*. In this context, we can easily conjecture the affinity between *li*, *fa*, and *shu*: they are all suggested as "objective" prescriptions or standards to guard against "subjective" and individual and thus, unreliable moral sentiments or qualities. However, this is their only similarity. As has been argued previously, *li* is not merely an instrumental, functional means to preserve social order, it is also a virtue-generating practice. In other words, through the thorough internalization of *li*-codes and *li*-activities, one becomes moral. *Li* is not only a normative prescription to enhance and preserve social-political order; it is also a practice to promote individual moral virtues. Accordingly, *li* is not just an objective, unalterable prescription imposed from above. It requires an individual's voluntary participation.

It can be further argued that, given the characteristic of *li* as the concrete embodiment of *dao,* the relation between *li* and the individual agent who practices it is not unilateral, but is rather interactive and "dialectical." That is, at the outset, a person has to comply with the given prescriptions of *li* without exception. Once that person thoroughly masters *li* and becomes morally virtuous and intellectually competent while still giving utmost respect to traditional *li,* he or she no longer blindly complies with the established prescriptions of *li,* but is able to add to, subtract from, or change *li* based on the sense of appropriateness in a particular situation.[36] The Xunzian philosophy that takes *li* as the central notion in moral theory is, thus, no exception to Schwartz' characterization of Confucianism: "In Confucianism we do have a vision in which the agency of living persons (albeit the agency of a vanguard elite) plays a dominant role in shaping society. Individual humans may achieve the highest norms of sociopolitical order or they may effectively outwit it."[37] On the contrary, *fa* and *shu* are completely functional means to control and govern a given society. There is, hence, no room for an individual to play a significant role in shaping society and no concern for the development of an individual's moral virtues: "In Legalism we will have a vision of a society in which 'objective' mechanisms of 'behavioral' control become automatic instruments for achieving well-defined sociopolitical goals."[38]

Xin and *Li*

Examining the differences between Xunzi and the Legalists, particularly Han Fei, I have hinted that Xunzi's notion of the autonomy of *xin* is crucial in preventing *li* from being a formal, coercive set of normative codes imposed from above. Without assuming the autonomy of *xin,* the gap between *li* and *fa* and *shu* would be much closer. What, then, is Xunzi's reason for letting the autonomous *xin* choose *li* as the most prominent educational and political tool for enhancing an individual's morality as well as political order? Reviewing our exploration of the notions of *xin* and *li* will clarify the relationship between them.

We argued that a proper understanding of *xin* required an examination of Xunzi's notions of *tian* and *xing;* because the contrast between these conceptions and *xin* is the underlying structure on which Xunzi builds his own philosophy against the contemporary philosophical trend of naturalism. We found that, for Xunzi, *tian* no longer exercises a direct influence on human affairs and it does not suggest a normative model for humans to emulate. That is, Xunzi strips *tian* of its anthropocentric, normative dimension. *Tian* in Xunzi's thought does not lack a religious element altogether, however. *Tian* is the source of all myriad things, and also an aspirational end for humankind. Thus, Xunzi can also be said to keep the traditional belief that humans can participate in the order of *tian*. What separates Xunzi from the naturalists is his emphasis on the way the trinity can be achieved; for Xunzi, the trinity between humans and *tian* and earth can be achieved only by exercising a person's distinctive faculties, not by mimicking the way of *tian*.

Humans are born with faculties given by *tian*. What faculty allows a person to pursue human ends and what faculty does not? Xunzi's answer lies in the distinction between the notions of *xin* and *xing;* while *xin* is the distinctive human faculty that must be actively employed in cultivating oneself and building society, *xing* represents passively responsive faculties through which a person cannot achieve morality and a harmonious society, and which, rather, leads a person to pursue selfish desires detrimental to the establishment of orderly society. Xunzi's statement that human *xing* is bad is one of the most clear examples of his explicit antipathy toward the naturalists, who seek the source of normative value in "naturalness" or "spontaneity." Spontaneous and natural tendencies in humans, namely human *xing*, are not reliable sources on which to nourish human morality and build an orderly society. They should be supervised and transformed by the autonomous faculty of *xin*. Only then can a person be morally achieved and bring about a harmonious society in which to participate in the order of *tian*.

Before examining the notion of the autonomy of *xin,* we pointed out the comprehensiveness of Xunzi's notion of *xin*. Because *xin* primarily refers to a bodily organ, it cannot escape having passively responsive properties that are included in the notion of *xing*. However, we have seen that Xunzi's autonomous *xin* does not conflict with the passive *xin*. Xunzi assumes the hierarchical structure within *xin;* that is, *xin* as the faculty of self-governance directs and supervises *xin* as the passively responsive faculties. Moreover, *xin,* having *xing*-like qualities, allows the sense of appropriateness to be included in it. This is a crucial point in Xunzi's moral psychology, because the sense of appropriateness, as we saw in discussing Xunzi's notion of *li,* provides one of the most fundamental reasons the Xunzian notion of morality is not arbitrary and hence not merely conventional. The intuitive sense of appropriateness is the basis upon which the autonomous *xin* deliberates and chooses a course of action in a given situation.

We have observed that a current Anglophone philosophical definition of the notion of autonomy as "the actual psychological condition of self-government" is in accord with the characteristics Xunzi confers *xin* as distinctive among human faculties. That is, the primary function of *xin* as the faculty of self-governance is critical or deliberative thinking to assess and guide first-order desires and emotions. This implies that *xin* is able to choose between the various sets of emotions and desires against the natural tendencies or inclinations inherent in humans. Xunzi calls the resultant choice or action "deliberative exertion." Persons, for Xunzi, can transform their natural inclinations only through the accumulation of "deliberative exertion." This "deliberative exertion" is based on knowledge gained through the combination of objective facts and subjective cognitive function. Xunzi puts equal stress both on *xin*'s cognitive function of confirming empirical knowledge and on the empirical source of knowledge. We noticed here that the most basic knowledge for Xunzi is the categorization of things that are the same and of those that are different.

"Deliberative exertion" posits two things: first, an agent has a volitional power that allows his or her critical thinking to be unaffected and unimpaired by desires and emotions. Second, the exercise of volition follows *xin*'s judgment of what is reasonable. The second assumption raises the question: Can there be an occasion on which *xin*'s judgment misleads the exercise of the volition of *xin?* Xunzi replies that there are abundant occasions on which persons misjudge things. This is due to *xin*'s preoccupation with a partial aspect of a thing. The remedy for this obsession or attachment is to recover *xin*'s qualities of emptiness, unity, and placidness, in order to see things in a comprehensive, holistic way. Xunzi calls this holistic perspective *dao*. From the point of view of *dao,* Xunzi asserts, we should choose *li* as our moral guide to develop our virtuous characters as well as our sociopolitical guide to build a harmonious society in which material needs and spiritual well-being can be fulfilled.

Now we seem able to plausibly anticipate Xunzi's response to the question of how this autonomous *xin* chooses *li,* which appears to be no more than a customary morality, as the best possible solution to moral self-cultivation and the establishment of an orderly society. First, there is an affinity between the sense of appropriateness and the knowledge of the sameness and the difference among things. The sense of appropriateness is basically the awareness of social division and hierarchy as a "natural" phenomenon in building a human society; some people are more apt to farm and others are more apt to trade; some people work hard to develop their moral virtues and others are lax in developing their virtuous characters. Those who are labeled noble or base are determined according to the degree of their moral cultivation. This categorization follows the categorization of things according to their sameness and their differences. That *xin*'s intuitive sense of appropriateness is in accord with the knowledge it gains through empirical data implies that *li,* which bases its codes and activities on the sense of appropriateness, is not arbitrarily invented, but carefully designed according to our cognitive capability to understand the world. *Li* is, after all, not merely conventional morality; although it is invented out of the need to cope with a disorderly sociopolitical situation, it is firmly grounded on *xin*'s ability to comprehend what is reasonable and appropriate. Given the reasonableness and appropriateness of *li,* it does not seems odd that the autonomous agent deems *li* a cogent way for self-cultivation and the establishment of an orderly society.

Second, we can point out the connection between Xunzi's assertion that persons should transform their natural tendencies and the notion of *li* as a "practice." Given the circumstances in ancient China, it would not be surprising that someone with an aptitude for deliberative thinking should find in *li* the best available resource to direct natural inclinations in a proper direction. An educational program to develop virtuous persons is not likely to be found in geometry or mathematics, but in *li* where one learns how to behave in a certain situation and how to refine and transform his or her desires and emotions appropriate to a given occasion. In other words, *li* can be deemed one of the best ways to transform first-order emotions and desires into second-order emotions and desires.[39] *Li* having the capacity to form second-order desires and emotions also turns out to be an important measure to preserve *xin*'s autonomous capacities, which should be free from the disruptive influences of first-order emotions and desires.

Li as a practice not only involves the transformation of first-order desires, it lays bare the character of *li* not as theoretical knowledge, but as practical, embodied knowledge. After all, Xunzi does not promotes *xin*'s capacity for abstract reasoning in order to find some transcendental truth or universal principle applicable to every situation and occasion, but *xin*'s "concrete rationality" to find a practical guide for cultivating a moral character that can flexibly adjust to changing circumstances without losing sight of the holistic picture. The following statement, in which Xunzi emphasizes the importance of practice in completing knowledge, is, thus, best understood in terms of the character of *li* as practical, concrete knowledge that requires an agent to internalize it through ceaseless practice:

> Not having heard something is not as good as having heard it; having heard it is not as good as having seen it; having seen it is not as good as knowing it; knowing it is not as good as putting it into practice . . . Hence, one who has heard about something but not seen it, even though he is broadly learned, will surely fall into error. He who has seen it but does not know it, although he has committed it to memory, will certainly be led astray. He who knows it but has not put it into practice, although he is well grounded in it, will certainly be reduced to beleaguered straits. One who has neither heard nor seen it, although by chance his actions should be fitting, will not be humane, for in a hundred attempts his way will produce a hundred failures. (24/8/102–105, Knoblock 8.11)

Finally, let us look at the relation between *xin* and *li* through the examination of how a sage-king who initiates the invention of *li* can become a sage-king without the knowledge of *li*. One clue to the understanding of this process is that human *xin* has the capacity to know the sense of appropriateness, that is, to see what is reasonable and what is in accordance with the order of the world. However, given that the sense of appropriateness is different from spontaneous moral inclinations in that it requires arduous intellectual and volitional endeavors, it is surely very difficult for an ordinary person to develop a morally virtuous and intellectually enlightened character against his or her disorderly natural dispositions without the aid of a specific and dependable guide. This, however, does not exclude the possibility that certain people are born with relatively modest natural dispositions as well as high intelligence and strong volition. These people, through numerous trial and error and by their *xin*'s capacity to exercise intellect and volition based on the sense of appropriateness, transform their raw dispositions into second-order dispositions. Consequently, they are able to envision a way that not only curbs and transforms first-order emotions and desires, but reflects the order of the world. They, then, initiate a project to give specific contents to that vision; finally, out of their thoughtful deliberation, *li* is invented. Xunzi succinctly calls this process "transforming natural dispositions and initiating deliberative activity" (*huaxingqiwei* 化性起偽) (87/23/28, Knoblock 23.2a). In this narration, we recognize that becoming a sage is closely linked to initiating or inventing *li*. The sages are those who themselves have experienced the taxing process of redirecting and changing their natural inclinations. As a result, it is natural for them to make their priority the invention of *li*, which takes into account the dual human psychological structure between *xing* and *xin*, as well as the order of natural phenomenon.

In sum, without the initiation of autonomous *xin*, *xing* can never be transformed, and, without the deliberative capacity of *xin*, *li* can never be invented. Once persons recognize that human psychological structure as well as the structure of nature is deeply reflected in *li*, they no longer see *li* as merely conventional custom or morality, but voluntarily adopt it as the best available moral guide by which to become virtuous persons and form a flourishing society.

Chapter 6

Naturalism and Autonomy

Introduction

When I set out to examine the autonomous character of the notion of *xin* in Xunzi, I maintained that the notion of the autonomy of *xin* offers a pivotal clue to understanding the nature of the Xunzian notion of morality, *li,* as conventional yet "objective," and that these notions of the autonomy of *xin* and *li* can best be understood as Xunzi's response to the "naturalistic" trend of his time. I also suggested that Xunzi's autonomous agent, in contrast to the Kantian notion of the autonomous agent, shapes morality that not only reflects natural order, but is sensitive to historical circumstances. My argument, so far, seems to have shown that *li* is not merely conventional because it is invented out of the sages' deliberations, which take into consideration both human psychology and the natural pattern of the world. In other words, *li*'s reasonableness is grounded on *xin*'s autonomous capacity to deliberate about things without being biased by emotions and desires and losing sight of a holistic picture. I also argued that since *li,* offering moral guidance for the autonomous agent, is the concrete embodiment of a holistic *dao*-perspective that encompasses ever-changing particulars, *li*-morality is more sensitive to historical changes than the Kantian morality, which is based on abstract and universalizable principles.,

However, to those who are familiar with the history of Western philosophy and the Western liberal tradition, the claim that *li* serves as central moral guidance for the autonomous agent sounds implausible, even contradictory. Thus, before concluding this study, a comparative perspective might be helpful to clarify the notion of the autonomy of *xin* in Xunzi. For this purpose, I use the Kantian notion of autonomy as the basis for a comparative study. Needless to say, Kant is considered one of the most important philosophers in shaping the Western philosophical understanding of autonomy. In fact, his ethics can be said to be built around the notion of a person as an autonomous agent. The comparison between Xunzi's notion of the autonomy of *xin* and the Kantian notion of autonomy will thus help us to bring into sharper focus the distinctive characteristics of the Xunzian notion of autonomy. This study of Kantian ethics will be confined to a narrow scope; that is, I will present a picture of Kantian ethics that is based on his earlier work, the *Groundwork of the Metaphysics of Morals,* rather than offer a detailed analysis of his later works, particularly the *Metaphysics of Morals*. There are two reasons for doing this. First, those who would be most perplexed about our employment of the notion of autonomy in exploring Xunzi's conception of *xin* would likely be those who have in mind the Kantian notion of autonomy based on the *Groundwork of the Metaphysics of Morals,* which, in modern Anglo-American philosophy, has been regarded as the standard work for understanding Kantian ethics.[1] Second, the purpose of this comparative study is not to explore Kantian ethics comprehensively, but to lay bare the characteristics of the Xunzian notion of autonomy, and, therefore, this picture of Kantian ethics, though one-sided, better serves to clarify the distinctive features of the Xunzian notion of autonomy.

This comparative study of the Xunzian and Kantian notions of autonomy will be carried out by situating Kantian autonomy in the context of the modern scientific worldview. This narrative structure will allow the comparison, more specifically, of Xunzi's notion of the autonomy of *xin* as a response to ancient Chinese naturalism with Kant's notion of autonomy as a response to the modern, mechanistic, scientific view of nature. This strategy of dealing with both the modern, scientific worldview and ancient Chinese naturalism may also be criticized for oversimplification. My generalizations may be accused, on the one hand, of having a far-reaching scope that tends to omit important particular cases that resist such generalizations and, on the other hand, of oversimplification because they overlook the internal tension or struggle within each tradition. However, one should not fail to notice the contribution of such generalizations, not only because they encourage more specific and nuanced studies, but also because they provide holistic pictures as well as useful starting points in approaching certain subjects. Particularly in this case, the generalizations about the modern scientific view of nature and the Chinese organicist worldview that are presented in the following sections seem to serve well as overviews of the backgrounds of the development of both Kantian ethics and ancient Chinese naturalism.

Background for Kant's Ethics

In Christine Korsgaard's brief summary of the history of Western metaphysics from Plato to Kant, there is an account of the transition of the major ethical ideas from excellence to obligation.[2] This is a revolutionary process, because the transition from the ethics of excellence to that of obligation involves a drastic change in the metaphysical assumptions about the world, value, and their relationship, in particular from teleology to mechanistic materialism. In the teleological metaphysical scheme shared by Plato and Aristotle, value and fact are inextricably intertwined; that is, seeking guidance for our lives is never separated from seeking the knowledge of what we really are, for what a thing is supposed to be is what a thing really is. It seems natural that this line of thinking entails "the idea of excellence" in the ethical realm; the endeavor to realize what you as a human being are supposed to be is nothing but the endeavor to be good at being what you really are.

The advent of the modern era, particularly in a philosophical sense, begins with the attempt to replace the teleological understanding of the world and human beings with mechanistic materialism. Rene Descartes is called the "father of modern philosophy" because he is a pioneer in "the movement away from a teleological or goal-directed conception of the natural world toward a more impersonal and mechanistic physics."[3] What, then, is the major force lending support to this movement? The development of mathematical, physical science seems undoubtedly to be one of the most important forces supporting the movement away from teleology toward mechanistic materialism. The physics of Galileo and Newton offer a concept of nature totally different from that of Aristotelean science. The major factors that distinguish the method of Galilean-Newtonian mechanical physics from that of Aristotle and late medieval science are said to be as follows: "(a) The pursuit of systematic observations and experiments; (b) The search for measurable quantities characteristic of observable events; (c) The search for exact, simple, and general mathematical relations between various measurable quantities; (d) The attempt to arrange the discovered mathematical laws in deductive systems along the lines of Euclid's geometry."[4] The huge success of this mechanical, mathematical method in its empirical and practical applications made the preceding Aristotelean-medieval outlook obsolete. Ever since, mathematical physics has become the model for scientific research. When "naturalism" is defined in a contemporary dictionary of philosophy as "the view that ultimately nothing resists explanation by the methods characteristic of the natural sciences,"[5] the method of mathematical physics is largely accepted as "the method characteristic of the natural sciences."[6]

The influence of Galilean-Newtonian science was enormous and, most profoundly, it drastically changed the view of nature. Nature was no longer seen to possess the Aristotelean teleological structure within which value and fact are interconnected. According to the above characterization of the distinctive method of Galilean-Newtonian science, in which objects for authentic scientific research were confined within the scope of quantifiable material things, nature came to be seen "as a vast field of lifeless objects governed by the mechanical laws of inertia and blind forces."[7] In such a world, there is no longer a natural basis for human values and concerns. It is in this context that Kant strives to find a place for value in the world. Korsgaard portrays Kant as someone who completes the revolution by the thesis that "reason—which is form—isn't in the world, but is something that we impose upon it."[8]

Kant developed his ethical ideas against the background of this modern, scientific worldview. Kant's first task was to demarcate the realm of the knowable from that of the unknowable. Saving the validity of Newtonian science from Humean skepticism was an indispensable first step for Kant in establishing his philosophical project. Kant was a Newtonian who fully accepted a materialistic, mechanistic view of nature, and securing the metaphysical basis for natural science would allow him to proceed to establish the proper realm of human ethical issues. In other words, a clear distinction between the natural realm and the human realm was needed to confirm the validity of natural science, on the one hand, and to establish the human ethical realm, on the other.[9] In his *Critique of Pure Reason,* Kant thus concentrated on the problem of the possibility of metaphysics, which he understood as philosophical knowledge that transcends the bounds of experience. For Kant, such knowledge is both synthetic and a priori.[10] Given Hume's argument that we cannot even prove the law of causality, one of the foundational principles of natural science, how could there be such knowledge that claims "necessary truths, which, as such, cannot be based on empirical evidence (their apriority), but which also claim more of their referents than can be derived from an analysis of their concepts (their syntheticity)"?[11] Moreover, given the antinomies that reason inevitably encounters when it ventures beyond experience in order to prove the traditional beliefs of God, immortality, and freedom, how could we philosophically deal with the most significant problems faced by those who want to lead their lives meaningfully? Kant suggested a new way of approaching these problems: that is, instead of thinking of our knowledge as conforming to a realm of objects, we think of objects as conforming to our ways of knowing. More specifically, the "forms of sensibility" in us are those through which objects are given to the mind in sensory experience, and the pure concepts or categories in us are those through which they are thought. Kant thus claimed that "we can know a priori of things only what we ourselves put into them."[12] This Copernican revolution in approaching epistemological problems of metaphysics, however, split the world into phenomena and noumena; since objects must appear to us in accordance with these sensible forms in order to be known, it follows that we can know them only as they appear, not as they may be in themselves. Accordingly, for Kant, human knowledge is limited to appearances or phenomena, whereas things-in-themselves, or noumena, are thinkable, but not actually knowable.

Kant's Deontological Ethics and the Notion of Autonomy

The scheme of "transcendental idealism" enabled Kant to secure the metaphysical basis of natural science by confining its applicability to the phenomenal world. Thus, the phenomenal world could still be seen as being governed by mechanistic, scientific principles and laws. Consider some prominent synthetic a priori principles that Kant infers from the method of a "transcendental deduction": Substance in nature remains permanent throughout all changes and every alteration has a cause. Kant, after all, did not totally break with either the Western metaphysical tradition or the Newtonian worldview. He merely suggested a new way of legitimatizing them.

Given the deterministic character of phenomena, how can there be room for freedom, the necessary condition for our ethical realm? As can be expected, Kant seeks a solution in the realm of noumena. For Kant, freedom is "a special kind of causality—first or spontaneous causality, unconditioned by any prior cause." Since the phenomenal world is temporal, causality as "temporal succession according to rule" applies to it, yet temporality cannot apply to the noumenal world, and thus, freedom, "a spontaneous causality, is possible, though not knowable,"[13] in the noumenal world. The human ethical realm is obtained by the division of the world into mechanistic, causal phenomena and unknowable, yet conceivable noumena. Once the freedom of will is saved from the phenomenal world, the question follows: "How would a free will with nothing constraining or guiding it determine its actions?" Kant answers that it is by "the moral law."[14] What kind of moral law is this and how can it regulate our actions? Kant postulates two characteristics of moral law: First, the moral law has to have moral necessity the way that natural laws hold necessarily in the physical universe. Second, the initiation of action, the will, occurs in response to desires as well as rational reasoning. Kant calls the rational source of the will "practical reason." Moral action, that is, actions motivated by the moral law, must originate from practical reason, not from any other dispositional tendencies. Since the faculty of practical reason has an inherent structure in the same way as the faculty of theoretical reason, it can impose "form on the givens we feel as desires."[15] This is how Kant conceives of humans as being able to have morality: they are "autonomous." What is prominent in this way of thinking is that Newtonian natural science, which is built around the notion of the necessity and universality of natural laws, still provides Kant with the standard or criterion for establishing human morality. J. B. Schneewind puts it this way: "Taking the activity of practical reason as the source of necessities that we impose on our willed behavior would show that these necessities are no more escapable than those that give structure to the physical world. This could therefore constitute our morality."[16]

Moral, autonomous agents are rational agents who can make their actions conform, not to desires or other psychological inclinations, but to reason. This entails that the central standard for the principles of morality should be "universalizability," because what reason allows to be rational cannot be bound by contingent factors such as historical circumstances or subjective desires. Thus, that someone is autonomous means that he or she is able to legislate universally valid moral laws and to impose those laws on him- or herself voluntarily. All other ways of legislating and adopting moral laws are considered "heteronomous." Only someone who "is subject only to laws given by himself but still universal" and who is "bound only to act in conformity with his own will"[17] can be called "autonomous." This notion of autonomy is closely linked to another central conception in Kant's ethics, the "categorical imperative." Whereas "hypothetical imperatives" are based on heteronomous motivations, the categorical imperative is an unconditional obligation that is possible only when the agent can bind his or her action out of his or her autonomous motivation, that is, when he or she gives the moral law to himself or herself.[18]

There are several notable points in this Kantian notion of autonomy. First, the autonomous agent is established purely on the "transcendental" level devoid of any experiential contents. Given Kant's emphasis on the foundational priority of "an autonomous will" in grounding the moral law, it seems unavoidable that no empirical elements are allowed in order for the agent to be completely autonomous. Because any empirical factors, such as human psychological inclinations or particular sociohistorical circumstances, are deemed contingent (and thus, heteronomous), the autonomous agent has to be the "transcendental subject."[19] Although the notion of the transcendental subject is first conceived as the epistemological ground for the unity of the self, it also provides Kant with a fitting basis for the self to be an autonomous agent who can make choices freely, "unconditioned by the contingencies of circumstances."[20] As the freedom of will is secured in the realm of noumena, the autonomy of the self can be secured only when we conceive of ourselves as transcendental subjects who are prior to and independent of experience. This leads to the second characteristic of Kantian moral philosophy. The thorough exclusion of empirical contents in the notion of autonomy implies that the moral laws that the autonomous agent legislates and by which he is bound are prior to and independent of any particular vision of the good. Insofar as the conception of the good involves various interests and ends, it cannot avoid empirical elements, and thus cannot avoid contingency. For Kant, only the thing that is good unconditionally is a "good will" or a "rational will" that enables the agent to conform with the moral law for no other reason than "for the sake of the law."[21] This way of establishing the foundational priority of the moral law is clearly opposed to any teleological and consequentialist attempts to base morality on the notion of "ends" or "consequences." Kantian moral philosophy is called "deontological ethics" because it gives priority to the obligation or duty to obey the moral law for its own sake regardless of any motivations to achieve good results. Third, the fundamental presupposition underlying Kantian deontological ethics, in spite of its claim that it does not depend on any empirical anthropology or psychology, is the belief that human beings are essentially rational. Without assuming the faculty of reason as the essential feature of human beings, we have no source from which to derive universally valid moral law (the "categorical imperative"), and no ground on which to legitimatize the authority of the moral law. Since the faculty of reason, for Kant, entails scientific necessity, universality and impartiality gained by complete detachment from personal emotions and desires, the notion of the autonomous moral agent in Kant seems to leave little room for any concern for particular individuals and circumstances[22] and seems to deny the positive role of emotions that can spontaneously move in a moral direction.[23]

In short, the Kantian autonomous person is a transcendental individual independent of sociohistorical circumstances and detached from his or her emotions and desires. In terms of this Kantian view of morality and its relation to autonomy, all other ways of establishing moral theories can be seen as lacking "the principle of autonomy," because they base their theories not on "a rational will," but on the observation of human psychological tendencies, the assumption of human nature, or other heteronomous sources. Why did Kant so tenaciously insist on a notion of autonomy that thoroughly excludes human psychological inclinations and a notion of morality completely independent of empirical elements? Korsgaard's narrative of the Western metaphysical tradition indicates that, by Kant's time, there was no longer a belief in the natural world as the source of value. In order to save morality from the world of hard, value-resistant, inert matter, Kant had to find morality in a human faculty (namely, the faculty of reason) to legislate universal moral laws, and in the human rational will, so that we might impose those laws on ourselves voluntarily.

Chinese Naturalism and Xunzi's Notion of the Autonomy of *Xin*

Several attempts have been made to characterize the ancient Chinese view of nature. Prominent among these is Joseph Needham's characterization of it as "organic naturalism."[24] Emphasizing the absence or underdevelopment of the notion of a supreme being in Chinese thought, which might produce "the concept of precisely formulated abstract laws" because of "the rationality of an Author of Nature, of being deciphered and re-stated," Needham expresses the Chinese worldview in the following way:

> The harmonious cooperation of all beings arose, not from the orders of a superior authority external to themselves, but from the fact that they were all parts in a hierarchy of wholes forming a cosmic pattern, and what they obeyed were the internal dictates of their own nature.[25]

In the similar vein, Frederick Mote also emphasizes the influence of the absence of "creation myth" on the shaping of the Chinese worldview:

> The basic point which outsiders have found so hard to detect is that the Chinese, among all peoples ancient and recent, primitive and modern, are apparently unique in having no creation myth; that is, they have regarded the world and man as uncreated, as constituting the central features of a spontaneous self-generating cosmos having no creator, god, ultimate cause or will external to itself.[26]

Both observers commonly point out the close connection between the absence of the idea of a supreme being in China and the Chinese view of nature as an organic whole or a spontaneous, self-generating unity. In this world, we can hardly find the rigid distinction between true reality and mere appearances or the significant rupture between nature and human beings. In Tu Wei-ming's locution, the idea of "the continuity of being" in which "all modalities of being are organically connected"[27] is one of the fundamental assumptions that permeates Chinese philosophical thinking.

In short, in contrast to the Galilean-Newtonian natural scientific view, which takes nature as lifeless, inert matter governed by mechanistic laws (and, thus, without intrinsic value), the Chinese organicist view sees nature as a self-generating, spontaneous process in which every particular being is organically interrelated. It thus seems natural that when philosophers look for the source of normativity, they take notice of the spontaneous way of nature. More specifically, in the case of Mencius, the foundation of morality is sought in natural human emotions. We should not confound this Mencian naturalism with

David Hume's ethical theory, which bases morality not on reason, but on sympathy. What drives Hume to approve of human sentiments as the source of morality is not his belief in the organic connectedness between natural human emotions and the natural world. It is his distrust of reason as "the slave of passions" that leads him to look for another source of morality. Hume, like Kant, is a modern Western philosopher who considers the world to be nothing but value-neutral, inert matter. On the contrary, for Mencius, the fact that humans have the emotional tendency to be affected by the suffering of others is directly related to the "naturalness" of worldly phenomena. Benevolent or compassionate emotions are as natural as water flowing downward. After all, for Mencius, "all the ten thousand things are there in me";[28] if we can thoroughly examine and cultivate our inner sources, namely *xin* and *xing*, we can also know *tian*.[29]

Though different in philosophical direction from Mencius, Zhuangzi also regards human beings as an organic part of the universe. Zhuangzi further pursues the character of nature as "self-so-ness (*ziran* 自然)," which can be rendered as "naturalness" or "spontaneity," and comes to conclude that all of the artificial (and thus nonnatural) habits of mind, cultural product, and human morality should be denied for humans to achieve "authentic personhood (*zhenren* 真人)" as members of the world. In short, the idea of "the continuity of being" underlies both the Mencian and Zhuangzian philosophies. They deem the main feature of nature, "naturalness" or "spontaneity," as the source of value, rather than characteristic of humanity such as historical culture or social norms. Thus, thinkers may be categorized as "naturalists" in spite of the difference in their philosophical orientations. One may questions whether this characterization of Mencius and Zhuangzi as "naturalists" does full justice to both philosophers; neither Mencius nor Zhuangzi ignores the importance of human agency in arriving at "achieved personhood." The idea of "achievement" may be said to have already been deeply embedded in the notion of sage or the authentic person. However, this study has focused on Xunzi's reading of both philosophers, and given their insufficient articulation of the relation between the role of human agency and the natural source of value, Mencius and Zhuangzi themselves seem to have given Xunzi grounds for his somewhat truncated reading of them.

What, then, is Xunzi's concern with Chinese naturalism and, particularly, the naturalistic tendency in the thought of Mencius and Zhuangzi? As has been emphasized, Xunzi's concern with naturalism is not with its underlying assumption about the world and its relation to humanity as "the organic whole" or "the continuity of being." As with Kant, who has no doubt about the traditional, Western, metaphysical assumptions such as the priority of permanence over change, Xunzi also accepts the traditional, Chinese view of the world as the whole of organically interrelated, constantly changing particulars, enabling humankind to arrive at a trinity with heaven and earth. What is problematic about naturalism for Xunzi is, rather, that the naturalists seem to undermine the importance of human effort even in building a flourishing, humane society. In other words, when the spontaneous way of nature and natural emotions are overemphasized as the sources of value, there seems to be insufficient room left for the active role of human agency in establishing a flourishing society and ultimately completing the trinity with heaven and earth.

In order to secure the importance of the role of human agency, Kant establishes the human ethical realm by separating it from the natural, phenomenal realm. Similarly, Xunzi has to clearly demarcate the human realm from the realm of *tian*. After identifying the natural realm in humans with the notion of *xing*, Xunzi goes on to articulate the notion of *xin* as the source of "autonomous" moral agency, which makes it possible to establish distinctive human morality that does not just follow the spontaneous way of nature unreflectively. In some respects, Xunzi's way of establishing human morality may appear similar to the way Kant builds his moral philosophy, despite the vast differences in their specific philosophical contents and agendas. Both Kant and Xunzi consider the task of their moral philosophy to be securing the ground of human morality differently from the way of nature; they both stress the importance of human agency in constructing morality. As a result, they both emphasize the role of the autonomy of *xin* or of the autonomous agent in establishing a human morality distinctive from the spontaneous way of nature and free from the law of causality. Also, both thinkers take the faculty of reflective or critical reasoning, which is not impeded by emotions and desires, to be the central constituent of the notion of autonomy.

However, when we encounter Xunzi's notion of *li* and Kant's theory of moral law, we could wonder what led them to take such different paths in their moral theories. One of the key differences between them undoubtedly comes from the fundamental divergence in their views of nature. For Xunzi, although persons should not emulate the way nature works, the ultimate goal of human achievement is still to form an organic whole with nature. The separation between the human realm and the natural realm is thus not ontological, but is didactic and explanatory to remind people that their work should be done in a distinctively human way. More significantly, for Xunzi, human morality, though constructed out of deliberative thinking, reflects the structure of the natural order. Accordingly, one of the pivotal reasons *li* is not just conventional morality lies in its isomorphic relation to the way things really are. Thus, the primary philosophical task, for Xunzi, is to underscore the role of human, constructive effort in establishing morality, and also to retain the continuity between human morality and the world in order to prevent human morality from becoming a totally arbitrary convention. Xunzi does not seem to have regarded this task as impossible, for he is, after all, a premodern philosopher who believes that value and fact, the human and the natural, are interconnected and mutually entailing.

On the contrary, the modern scientific view of nature leads Kant to construct human morality in the realm of noumena, completely independent of the spatiotemporal, natural world. The natural world, for Kant, is just matter that is mechanically governed by natural laws. Thus, Kantian morality has to be built on the ground of a strict ontological distinction between the human, ethical realm and the natural, phenomenal realm. Put another way, Kantian morality is thoroughly an artificial construction, without any connection with the natural realm. How, then, can Kant avoid the conventionality or arbitrariness of morality? This requires Kant to construct a moral law that relies on the notions of universality and necessity, which do not, and must not, allow any contingent elements. In other words, the strict, ontological separation between the human, ethical realm and the natural, phenomenal realm leads Kant to take the central features of the laws of natural sciences, namely universality and necessity, as the models for moral law, in order to prevent the moral law from being contingent and arbitrary. In sum, in order to save the ethical realm from the phenomenal world, where deterministic natural laws govern, and to establish a moral law that is impervious to contingency and arbitrariness, the transcendental realm is, for Kant, the only fitting sphere in which the individual can become an autonomous moral agent.

The difference between Xunzi's and Kant's notions of autonomy and morality can be examined based on the foregoing analysis of the differences in their views of nature. The examination of the apparent affinity between Xunzi and Kant in their negative views of human, natural dispositions can offer useful guidance in exploring the distinctive characters of the notions of autonomy and morality in their moral systems.

As has been observed, one of the most fundamental reasons Kant rejects emotions and desires as the ground for morality is that he sees these human, psychological dispositions as contingent, empirical facts that cannot entail the necessity required by the moral law. For Kant, if natural, psychological tendencies are regarded as the foundational source of morality, then, "it is a matter of happenstance whether or not someone is bound by any moral necessity."[30] The empirical character of psychological dispositions also entails incompatibility with morality, because morality posits the possibility of a free will, which belongs not to deterministically governed, empirical phenomena, but to transcendental noumena. Thus, the only feasible candidate for the source of morality is the thoroughly disembodied faculty of impersonal reason, not any other human faculties associated with the physical body. As a consequence, the autonomous agent in Kant relies solely on the faculty of reason completely detached from psychological inclinations, and this in turn ensures the impartiality and universality of the moral law legislated by the autonomous agent. In short, since the fundamental structure of Kantian transcendental idealism is established on the basis of the firm dichotomy between empirical phenomena and transcendental noumena, it is, for Kant, unavoidable that the notions of autonomy and morality are based on the strict distinction between reason and emotions/desires.

In contrast, although Xunzi, like Kant, also rejects natural dispositions as the basis of morality, he sees no difficulty in admitting these psychological tendencies are the components of autonomous agency. *Xin,* is, for Xunzi, never a disembodied faculty in humans. Because *xin* refers, not to an abstract faculty, but to a human bodily organ, it is not odd that, for Xunzi, it has both the capacities of deliberation and volition and the faculties of emotions and desires. Accordingly, Xunzi's negative position toward psychological dispositions is limited to the claim that they can offer the basis for morality. Human natural dispositions are an unreliable, and even destructive source of morality. Thus, persons need to refine and transform natural, psychological inclinations by exercising the autonomous faculties of *xin:* reflective thinking and volitional power. At the same time, Xunzi gives equal stress to the indispensability of natural dispositions as raw material without which deliberative activities cannot be initiated. Insofar as dispositional tendencies such as emotions and desires are refined and transformed into second-order dispositions, they become necessary ingredients for a person to reach an autonomous, achieved personhood. Xunzi's achieved person is, as has been cited, not different from Confucius, who at the age of seventy, could "follow what his *xin* desires without overstepping the boundaries."[31] However, what should not be missed here is that Xunzi also pays careful attention to the way dispositional tendencies may disrupt impartial, holistic moral judgment. Xunzi's exposition of *xin*'s capacities to be empty, unitary, and placid clearly shows his concern with the negative effect psychological dispositions have on making moral judgment. We must also recall that, for Xunzi, these capacities of *xin* are not extraordinary or mysterious qualities that enable persons to acquire a transcendental viewpoint; rather, they are the specific attributes of deliberate thinking by which to attain a *dao*-perspective.

Accordingly, that someone is autonomous, for Xunzi, means not that he or she posits him- or herself as the transcendental subject protected from all impure bodily (and thus, empirical) contingency, but that, while recognizing his or her embodiedness, he or she strives to gain a *dao*-perspective by fully exercising the autonomous faculties of *xin*. The *dao*-perspective does not, after all, offer a universalizable maxim or principle, but rather yields a holistic vision in which concrete and contingent particulars should be taken into account.[32]

Seen in this context, it is not difficult to understand why Xunzi views *li* as the best guide by which persons should exercise their autonomous capacities. For Xunzi, a person does not have to be a transcendental subject to be autonomous. All he or she has to do is to make an effort to keep his or her autonomous faculties from being dominated by natural dispositions and to exercise these faculties in making judgments and cultivating him- or herself. What he or she discovers in this process is that there is already an excellent guide for him or her: *li*. *Li* provides the aesthetically sophisticated, expressive forms necessary to give vent to natural emotions and desires and transform them into second-order dispositions that are conducive to exercising autonomous capacities. In other words, *li* does not amount to the Kantian moral law, which leaves little room for recognizing human, bodily, dispositional elements; rather, *li* is properly seen as a set of detailed prescriptions for appropriate behavior that serve as the medium to connect the natural dispositions with the autonomous faculties of *xin* within the hierarchical structure of *xin*. Further, given the simple fact that *li* is a major component of Chinese cultural heritage in the time of Xunzi, it is not likely that Xunzi neglects the contingent element of *li* entailed by its historical character. Although Xunzi does not explicitly elaborate on the historical dimension of *li*, since language, for Xunzi, reflects the changing circumstances of a given historical time, *li* as the concrete embodiment of *dao* should also be flexible enough to reflect the vicissitudes of the times.

In conclusion, the differences between Kant and Xunzi in their notions of autonomy and morality can be summarized in the following manner: for Kant, the autonomous agent must be the transcendental subject to guard against the possibility that the agent falls victim to deterministic laws that govern the empirical, phenomenal world. Ironically, the empirical element entails not only determinism, but also contingency. Since the assumption of a noumenal world makes possible not only the legitimacy of deterministic causal laws, but also the feasibility of a free will that ensures the ethical realm, the empirical element can be seen either as deterministic or as contingent, depending on whether we take the perspective of determinism or that of moral law. Put differently, that we follow the direction of desires or emotions in our action may be interpreted in either way; either deterministic causal laws govern our actions or we act utterly out of contingent motivations. Since the moral law requires moral necessity, Kant sees action arising out of psychological dispositions or any other considerations of empirical matter as contingent. From the standpoint of the notion of moral law, practical reason or rational will remains not only the sole viable candidate for the source of morality, but also the only component of the autonomous agent. Thus, it is quite natural that the autonomous agent in Kant is the transcendental subject, who relies on nothing but impersonal, disembodied reason in legislating the moral law, and that this moral law, the categorical imperative, gives little consideration to concrete, sociohistorical circumstances or to particular individuals' psychological dispositions. Put simply, only noumenal selves, who do not have any connection to concrete, embodied selves living in the specific sociohistorical time and place, seem to inhabit the Kantian "kingdom of ends."

On the contrary, since Xunzi's autonomous agent is an embodied self that firmly situates him- or herself in a concrete, sociohistorical context, he or she seems to have little reason to take abstract, universalizable, moral principle as guidance for his or her moral life. Instead, *li,* which is continuous with the pattern of natural phenomena and bridges the past with the present through respect for contingent, historical conditions, serves as a better guide for refining emotions and desires to be in accordance with deliberative thinking and judgment and to render one a constructive participant in shaping a flourishing society. It is thus, for Xunzi, quite natural that the autonomous faculties of *xin* lead a moral agent to see *li* as offering the most reliable guidance for self-cultivation and for building a sound society.

Chapter 7

Xunzi in the History of Chinese Philosophy

Introduction

For the greater part of the history of Chinese philosophy, until the recent reappraisal of Xunzi and Mencius by Chinese Marxist scholars,[1] Xunzi's philosophy has not elicited as much support as that of Mencius. Although it is often pointed out that Xunzi's philosophy played a crucial role in shaping Han Learning (*hanxue* 漢學),[2] it is also true that it was not until the ninth century that the first extant commentarial work on the *Xunzi* by Yang Liang appeared.[3] As is well known, the rise of neo-Confucianism in the Song dynasty (960–1279) and its subsequent establishment as the official orthodoxy in the Ming dynasty (1368–1644), had a great impact on the assessment of Mencian and Xunzian philosophy throughout this period; while Mencius's status as the authentic heir of Confucius was solidified, Xunzi was deemed a philosopher who had not truly understood the spirit of Confucius. The apparent reason for the neo-Confucians' lower evaluation of Xunzi is well documented; they assert that Mencius's thesis that human *xing* is good is the correct understanding of human natural dispositions, a thesis that Xunzi did not understand.[4]

During the Qing dynasty (1644–1911), the last dynasty of imperial China, we see the reverse of the metaphysical trend of Song-Ming neo-Confucianism; Qing Confucian scholars preferred Han Learning to Song-Ming neo-Confucianism as a more concrete and historically reliable source from which to derive guidance for Confucian self-cultivation and establishing social order. Thus, during the Qing period, it is not surprising that *li* (ritual, 禮) again surfaced as a central notion in Confucian ethical and political discourse,[5] and that there was a surge of interest in Xunzi's philosophy, at the same time.[6] However, this does not mean that Xunzi overtook Mencius in status during the Qing period. Ever since Zhu Xi chose the *Mencius* as one of the core Confucian classics, namely "the Four Books (*Analects, Mencius,* the *Doctrine of the Mean,* the *Great Learning*)," [7] it never lost its status as an essential Confucian canon. However, the *Xunzi* was never considered one of the Confucian canons, even during the Qing. It is thus not an overstatement to say that, throughout the history of Chinese philosophy, up until fairly recent times, Xunzi has not been given remotely as much attention as Mencius.

Li Zehou's View of Chinese Philosophy

What was the reason for this relative devaluation or neglect of Xunzi compared to the high esteem given to Mencius in traditional Confucianism? Was it simply what neo-Confucians suggested—that Xunzi did not fully appreciate natural, human, moral dispositions? Or was it historical circumstances such as the institutionalization of the Confucian educational curriculum that excluded Xunzi? If both the historical explanation and the tendentious account given by neo-Confucians are unsatisfactory, is there a more philosophically plausible reason? The overview of the history of Chinese philosophy provided by Li Zehou offers a framework around which an answer to this question might be constructed.[8]

According to Li, what makes traditional Chinese philosophy distinct is that all schools of Chinese thought "ascribe formidable power to the subject."[9] Thus, the "unity of heaven and mankind (*tianren heyi* 天人合一)," one of the most famous slogans and main tenets of almost all major Chinese philosophical schools, turns out to express infinite confidence in the transformative power of "the purified moral will"[10] of human agency, rather than to emphasize the equal weight of both subjective, human agency and the objective, natural world in pursuing a harmonious relationship between them; we may call the idea of empowering the moral subject with formidable transformative powers over nature "subjective volitionism."[11] In this view, the "naturalism" that is characterized as a distinct Chinese philosophical idea is nothing but "subjective volitionism" in disguise, because the belief in the organic relation between the natural world and humankind turns out only to provide a cosmological ground for the transformability of the natural world by the unmediated moral will of human agency. Li Zehou argues that this "volitionistic" idea plays a crucial role in shaping mainstream Confucianism from Confucius to Mencius to Wang Yangming, which promotes internal self-cultivation as the source of moral will that could exercise transformative powers over the malleable, natural world. In this respect, it is natural that Li sees Xunzi as an exceptional ancient Chinese philosopher who emphasizes "a struggle between human need and nature."[12] That Xunzi takes pains to make clear the "distinction between *tian* and humankind (*tianrenzhifen* 天人之分)," according to Li, shows that, in Xunzi's thought, "human culture depends on humankind's ability to combat nature and force it to provide humankind with the means of survival."[13]

Humankind and Nature in Xunzi's Philosophy

If Li Zehou's characterization of Xunzian philosophy is qualified appropriately, it does not seem difficult to infer from Li's overview of Chinese philosophy a plausible explanation for the reason Xunzi was shunned from mainstream Confucianism. Let me first differentiate my view of Xunzian philosophy, particularly Xunzi's idea of the distinction between *tian* and humankind, from Li's understanding of Xunzi. As has been emphasized, I do not think that Xunzi aims to break with the traditional, organicist worldview and set up an "antagonism between subject and object."[14] Given his emphasis on the establishment of a trinity between humankind and heaven and earth as the ultimate achievement of human morality and culture, and the way he justifies human morality and *li* as nonarbitrary, it seems unlikely that Xunzi views nature as something to combat and only as "the means for survival." To understand Xunzi's emphasis on the distinction between *tian* and humankind—as calling attention to the difference between the way nature works and the way humans should establish their morality—seems more plausible than to see it as underscoring the strict, ontological separation between the human and the natural spheres. In other words, it is not that Xunzi does not pursue the idea of the separation between humankind and nature consistently, but that he attempts to ground the unity of humankind and nature on the separation between them; for Xunzi, as long as people attempt to imitate the way of nature unreflectively or think of human morality as seamlessly connected to the natural world, it is hopeless to expect them to arrive at ultimate harmony with the natural realm. Only after recognizing the distinctive human faculties by which to transform natural dispositions and build a humane society, can persons form a trinity with heaven and earth.

In spite of my disagreement with Li's interpretation of Xunzian philosophy, Li's insightful schematization of Chinese philosophy offers the recognition that the devaluation of Xunzi could have been related to the "volitionistic" tendency of mainstream Confucianism, which bases its cosmological ground on Chinese naturalism. Put differently, Xunzi's attempt to build human culture and morality on the grounds of the distinction between *tian* and humankind could have been seen as a dangerous one, which negates a cosmological ground for the establishment of the "volitionistic" moral subject. The neo-Confucians' criticism of Xunzi is based on the latter's assertion that human, natural dispositions are bad. Apparently, this seems to have little connection to Xunzi's position regarding the relationship between *tian* and humankind. However, by taking a closer look at the remark that Zheng I, one of the leading Song neo-Confucians, makes about Xunzi's thesis of the badness of human *xing*, it will become clear how much weight neo-Confucians give to the cosmological implication of the thesis of human *xing:*

> Mencius was correct in saying that a person's *xing* is good. Even Xunzi and Yang Xiong failed to understand human *xing* . . . Badness is due to capacity. Human *xing* is the same as 'cosmic coherence (*li* 理),'[15] and 'cosmic coherence' is the same from the sage-emperors Yao and Shun to the common persons in the street.[16]

In this view, the reason human *xing* has to be good is that it is directly connected to "cosmic coherence." Once a direct connection between human *xing* and cosmic order is established, it is not much of a leap to endow the human agent with formidable transformative powers over the objective world. On the contrary, if we assume that human, innate tendencies are not reliable sources by which to form a harmonious relationship with nature, we not only have to take an indirect route in connecting humankind with the objective natural world, but cannot assume that the transformation of reality can be achieved solely by virtue of the meditative, inner cultivation of the moral subject. In other words, once we distinguish the human, ethical realm, in which a given "nature" in humankind is regarded as an unreliable guide for human morality, from the realm of nature whose working manner is supposed to be different from that of humans, the whole cosmological basis on which transforming power over the objective, natural world is conferred on the moral subject would be difficult to sustain.

In short, for mainstream Confucians, the Xunzian way of establishing the continuity between humankind and the natural world is not only far less favorable than the Mencian, it is also a dangerous attempt to shatter the foundation of the "volitionistic" moral subject.

It seems ironic that Xunzi's attempt to bring into sharper focus the importance of the constructive role of human agency in achieving ultimate harmony between humankind and the natural world leads him to oppose a "subjective volitionistic" position. This becomes apparent through a further articulation of the differences between Xunzian philosophy and Chinese volitionism in dealing with the role of human agency and its relationship with the objective world. Since subjective volitionism posits that human morality is continuous with natural *dao* or *li* 理 and that all the issues regarding the relationship between humankind and the natural world can be reduced to the cultivation of moral will within human agency, the objective world tends to be so malleable as to be absorbed into the moral subject. That is, the sphere of the objective world is so reduced that everything depends on the inner self-cultivation of the moral subject. On the contrary, Xunzian philosophy first makes clear the difference between the way of humankind and that of nature, and suggests that the only way for humans to achieve a harmonious relation with nature is by transforming given, natural dispositions into second-order dispositions and by learning and practicing the external morality constructed deliberately by the sages. In other words, for Xunzi, the subjective volitionism that confers immense power on the moral subject and renders the objective natural world infinitely malleable is not the proper way for persons to pursue the relationship between humankind and the natural world. It is the other side of naturalism that confounds the realm of humans with that of nature. Unless people first recognize the human psychological structure and respect the distinctive way nature works, they cannot even set out to pursue the harmonious relationship between humans and nature. The continuity between humankind and nature is just not given, it is achieved by the human construction of morality and culture.

When comparing Xunzi with Kant, I emphasized the different views of nature against which they each developed the notions of autonomy and morality. The major difference between them was that, while Kant, in pursuing human morality, firmly separated the human ethical realm from the natural realm at the ontological level, Xunzi's distinction between humankind and *tian* was practical and didactic, rather than ontological. For Xunzi, humans must recognize that ultimate harmony with the natural realm is achieved only in a distinctively human way, which should not be confounded with the way of nature. In contrasting Xunzi with the Chinese "volitionists," it becomes apparent that the difference between them rests on their different ways of establishing the connection between the human and natural realms. Whereas Xunzi sees the distinction between the way of human beings and that of nature as a necessary prerequisite for pursuing a harmonious relationship between the two, the volitionists take for granted the continuity between humans and nature and thus reduce the natural realm to the transformable object of subjective, human, moral cultivation.

In short, Xunzi is different from both Kant and the Chinese volitionists. Compared with a modern Western philosopher, Xunzi is still a premodern Chinese philosopher who believes in the fundamental continuity between the human realm and the natural realm and in the mutual entailment of fact and value. Within the Chinese philosophical tradition, however, he is unique in his insistence that the continuity between nature and humans is not given but "achieved" only by virtue of paying due respect to the distinctive way of humans, which does not take the way of nature as the model for morality and constructing a sound society.

It is unfortunate that the Xunzian approach to the relationship between humankind and the natural world was not fully appreciated and accepted by the later Confucian tradition. The naturalistic trend that developed into subjective volitionism, as Li Zehou points out, was a great obstacle to the modernization of China; that is, the volitionistic tradition that emphasizes the transformation of reality purely by virtue of inner moral cultivation, overlooking "the reality of nature's resistance to human intervention,"[17] was one of the crucial reasons that the modernization of China, which entailed scientific and technological development, was delayed.[18] If Xunzian philosophy were fully incorporated into mainstream Confucianism, the Confucian tradition would have paid much more attention to the way the natural world actually works, and generated a more realistic vision by which the Chinese people could treat human ethical issues as well as the relationship between humankind and the natural world in a less one-sided and idealistic way. While it is uncertain whether the Xunzian tradition, with its focus on human affairs, might have encouraged the development of science and technology, it would at least have been less disadvantageous to the modernization of China than subjective volitionism.

Notes

Chapter 1. Introduction

1. Xunzi is generally known as Xun Qing 荀卿, and his full name is Xun Kuang 荀況. According to John Knobock, Xunzi was born about 310 B.C.E., lived a long time, and probably saw the unification of states by the Qin before he died. See John Knoblock, *Xunzi: A Translation and Study of the Complete Works,* vol.1 (Stanford: Stanford University Press, 1989), pp. 3–35.

2. See Antonio S. Cua, *Ethical Argumentation: A Study in Hsun Tzu's Moral Epistemology* (Honolulu: University of Hawaii Press, 1985); Paul R., Goldin, *Rituals of the Way: The Philosophy of Xunzi* (Chicago: Open Court, 1999); Philip J. Ivanhoe, "A Happy Symmetry: Xunzi's Ethical Philosophy," *Journal of the American Academy of Religion* 59:2 (Summer), 309–322; Ivanhoe, "Human Nature and Moral Understanding in *Xunzi*," *International Philosophical Quarterly* 34:2 (1994), 167–175; David S. Nivison, "Xunzi on Human Nature," *The Ways of Confucianism: Investigations in Chinese Philosophy,* Bryan W. Van Norden, ed. (Chicago: Open Court, 1996), pp. 123–141; Nivison, "Hsun Tzu and Chuang Tzu," *Chinese Texts and Philosophical Contexts: Essays Dedicated to Angus C. Graham*, ed., Henry Rosemont, Jr. (Chicago: Open Court, 1991), pp. 129–142; Jonathan W. Schofer, "Virtues in Xunzi's Thought: Issues in Comparative Analysis," *The Journal of Religious Ethics* 21 (1993), 117–136; Bryan W. Van Norden, "Mengzi and Xunzi: Two Views of Human Agency," *International Philosophical Quarterly* 32:2 (1992), 161–184; Lee H., Yearley, "Hsun Tzu on the Mind: His Attempted Synthesis of Confucianism and Daoism," *Journal of Asian Studies* 39 (1980), 465–480. Several articles mentioned above are included in the recently published book, *Virtue, Nature, and Moral Agency in the Xunzi,* ed., T. C. Kline III and Philip J. Ivanhoe (Indianapolis: Hackett Publishing Company, 2000). A useful bibliography of scholarship on Xunzi in English is also contained in this volume.

3. Nivison, "Hsun Tzu and Chuang Tzu," pp. 129–130.

4. Throughout this study, I will leave several important Chinese philosophical terms untranslated. Aside from the usual difficulty in finding exact English terms to correspond to the Chinese, one reason for doing this is that it would cause less confusion than rendering the same terms differently according to their contexts, which is

inescapable in translating Chinese philosophical terms. I will, nonetheless, try to make the terms comprehensible in English by inserting commonly employed English translations in parenthesis whenever the term first appears and when it seems unclear only using the romanization.

5. I am aware that the term, *autonomy*, carries Western cultural baggage. However, the concept of autonomy as a psychological condition of self-governance in a contemporary philosophical sense captures well Xunzi's notion of *xin* as the supervisor over other human faculties such as emotions and desire, as well as his emphasis on deliberation as the key function of *xin*. Hence, if restricted to this narrow psychological sense, it seems possible to adopt the term *autonomy* for the characterization of Xunzi's notion of *xin* without invoking assorted unwanted associations. In a similar vein, Antonio Cua has already employed "the notion of the autonomy of mind" in discussing Xunzi's concept of *xin*. However, he does not focus on the notion of the autonomy of *xin* as the central topic in understanding Xunzi's moral psychology and ethics to the extent that I do here. Particularly see Cua, *Ethical Argumentation,* pp. 138–145. For a further discussion of Xunzi's notion of autonomy in comparison with the Kantian notion, see chap. 6.

6. My position is close to that of Michael O. Hardimon in his exploration of Hegel's social philosophy. See Michael O. Hardimon, *Hegel's Social Philosophy: The Project of Reconciliation* (Cambridge: Cambridge University Press, 1994), pp. 8–10.

7. Knoblock, *Xunzi,* vol.1–3 (Stanford: Stanford University Press, 1989–1994).

8. Burton Watson, *Hsün Tzu: Basic Writings* (New York: Columbia University Press, 1963).

9. *A Concordance to Hsün Tzu.* Harvard-Yenching Institute Sinological Index Series, Supplement no. 22 (Beijing: Harvard-Yenching Institute, 1950).

Chapter 2. Background

1. For a detailed analysis of the relationship between Xunzi and the Legalists, particularly Han Fei, see 5.4.1.

2. Zhu Xi puts it this way: "We [Confucians] consider the mind [*xin*] and principle [cosmic coherence, *li* 理] as one but they [Buddhists] consider the mind and principle as two . . . From their point of view, the mind is empty and is without principles, while from our point of view, although the mind is empty, all the principles are complete in it." Wing-Tsit Chan, *A Source Book in Chinese Philosophy* (Princeton: Princeton University Press, 1973), p. 648.

3. It is true that throughout the *Xunzi,* the Mohists are mentioned most frequently as the objects of harsh criticism. The most important reason we take the naturalists as Xunzi's main rivals rather than the Mohists is that Xunzi's distinction between *xing* and *xin,* and his emphasis on *li,* and *wei* (deliberative exertion), considered a main philosophical theme throughout Xunzi's philosophy, are most likely to be intended for the criticism of naturalism, not of Mohism.

4. A recent controversy surrounding the problem of whether or not *xing* can be rendered as "human nature" enhances our philosophical sensitivity to the translation of key Chinese philosophical terms. Relevant articles are as follows: A. C. Graham, "The Background of the Mencian Theory of Human Nature," in *Studies in Chinese Philosophy and Philosophical Literature* (Singapore: Institute of East Asian Philosophies, 1986), 7–66. Roger T. Ames, "The Mencian Conception of *Ren xing* 人性: Does it Mean 'Human Nature'?," in Rosemont, Jr., ed., *Chinese Texts and Philosophical Contexts*, pp. 143–178. Irene Bloom, "Mencian Arguments on Human Nature (*Jen-Hsing*)" *Philosophy East & West* vol. 44, no. 1, Jan. 1994, 19–53. Kwong-loi Shun, *Mencius and Early Chinese Thought* (Stanford: Stanford University Press, 1997), 180–231.

5. D. C. Lau, trans., *Mencius* (London: The Penguin Group, Penguin Books, 1970), bk. 2, part A, chap. 6, pp. 82–83.

6. Lau, *Mencius*, bk. 4, part B, chap. 19, p. 131.

7. Lau, *Mencius*, bk. 6, part A, chap. 6, p. 163.

8. Lau, *Mencius*, bk. 6, part A, chap. 8, pp. 164–165.

9. Lau, *Mencius*, bk. 7, part A, chap. 21, p. 186.

10. Lau, *Mencius*, bk. 6, part A, chap. 15, p. 168.

11. Manyul Im defines the Perfectibility Model as follows: "Full human moral development requires cultivation to perfection of the capacities involved in moral virtue. Such cultivation requires habituation or practice so that the dispositions of these capacities can go from an untutored deficient or excessive state to the morally mature state in which they can effectively motivate a person to feel and act in the appropriate and best ways." Manyul Im, "Emotional Control and Virtue in the *Mencius*," *Philosophy East & West* 49, no. 1, 1999, 10. Im's definition of "the Perfectibility Model" is very Aristotelian, and he actually opposes this model in interpreting the Mencian moral psychology. He instead proposes "the Natural Developmental Model," which emphasizes "the naturalness and completeness of moral emotions." Accordingly, Im insists that, in Mencian moral psychology, cultivation of emotions is not required. He seems to go too far in defending his interpretation of Mencius's moral theory against the Aristotelian Perfectibility Model.

12. Benjamin I. Schwartz, *The World of Thought in Ancient China* (Cambridge: the Belknap Press of Harvard University Press, 1985), 273.

13. See A. Ç. Graham, trans., *Chuang-Tzu: The Inner Chapters, A Classic of Tao* (London: An Inprint of HarperCollins *Publishers*, Mandala, 1986), chap. 4, p. 69, and Burton Watson, trans., *The Complete Works of Chuang Tzu* (New York: Columbia University Press, 1968), chap. 4, p. 58.

14. See Lee Yearley, "Hsün Tzu on the Mind: His Attempted Synthesis of Confucianism and Taoism," *Journal of Asian Studies* 39, no. 3, 1980, 468–473.

15. See Watson, *Chuang Tzu,* chap. 5, p. 69, and chap. 13, pp. 142, 144.

16. See Watson, *Chuang Tzu,* chap. 4, p. 58, and chap. 19, p. 206.

17. Watson, *Chuang Tzu,* chap. 4, p. 57.

18. Graham, *Chuang-Tzu,* chap. 19, p. 138. Waton, *Chuang Tzu,* chap. 19, 206.

19. Watson, *Chuang Tzu,* chap. 13, p. 142.

Chapter 3. The Notions of *Tian* and *Xing* in *Xunzi*

1. I borrow this term from Yearley. See Yearley, "Hsün Tzu on the Mind," pp. 465–468.

2. The third and fifth meanings of *tian* have produced a great deal of controversy, which usually centers on the question of whether the wording such as "fatalistic" and "principle" can be regarded as correct rendition of some aspects of *tian* and whether those characterizations imply that *tian* has any transcendental facet. For a recent attempt to criticize this tendency, especially among the Western sinologists, to seek a transcendental element not only in the concept of *tian* but also in the ancient Chinese philosophy in general, see Hall and Ames, *Anticipating China* (Albany: State University of New York, 1995). Concerning the notion of *tian,* see pp. 186–187, 199.

3. Fung Yu-lan, *A History of Chinese Philosophy,* vol. 1 (Princeton: Princeton University Press, 1952), p. 31.

4. Robert Eno, *The Confucian Creation of Heaven* (Albany: State University of New York Press, 1990), Edward J. Machle, *Nature and Heaven in the Xunzi* (Albany: State University of New York Press, 1993).

5. Eno, *The Confucain Creation of Heaven,* pp. 132–133. See also ibid., pp. 154–169.

6. A. C. Graham, *Disputers of the Tao: Philosophical Argument in Ancient China* (La Salle: Open Court Publishing Company, 1991), p. 239.

7. Machle, *Nature and Heaven in Xunzi,* p. 2.

8. In rendering the "*tianlun*" chapter, I have also consulted Eno's and Machle's translation. See Eno, "Hsun Tzu: Treatise on T'ien [Tian] (Appendix C)," in *The Confucian Creation of Heaven,* pp. 198–204, and Machle, "Translation and Commentary," in *Nature and Heaven in the Xunzi,* pp. 77–134.

9. See Eno, *The Confucian Creation of Heaven,* p. 132, Graham, *Disputers of the Tao,* p. 235, and Schwartz, *The World of Thought in Ancient China,* p. 309.

10. Graham, *Disputers of the Tao,* p. 235.

11. It is noteworthy that Xunzi deliberately appropriates Zhuangzi's term, "a consummate person (*zhiren* 至人)" and his expression of the division between *tian* and mankind: "He who knows what it is that *tian* does, and knows what it is that man does, has reached the peak (*zhi* 至). Knowing what it is that *tian* does, he lives with *tian.* Knowing what it is that man does, he uses the knowledge of what he knows to help out the knowledge of what he doesn't know, and lives out the years that *tian* gave him without being cut off midway—this is the perfection of knowledge." Watson, *Chuang Tzu,* chap. 6, p. 77. Later in the same chapter, Zhuangzi says that the perfect

man is someone who can act "as a companion of *tian*" as well as "a companion of man." Watson, *Chuang Tzu,* chap. 6, p. 80.

12. Lau, *Mencius,* bk. 7, part A, chap. 1, p. 182.

13. As Knoblock points out, "the doctrine of the Triad 參, a balance between Man, Heaven and Earth" "antedates Xunzi" and was generally known in Xunzi's time. It seems that as Xunzi accepts the doctrine of the triad as one of the central themes in his philosophy, he adopts the binominal term heaven and earth (天地 *tiandi*), rather than the singular term, *tian,* to express the doctrine. See Knoblock, *Xunzi,* vol. I, p. 70.

14. According to Li Disheng, the first characterization of *xing* refers to the biological instincts such as eating and sex, and the second to the faculties of sense organs such as seeing and hearing. See Li Disheng, *Xunzi jishi* (Taibei: Xuesheng Shuju, 1979), pp. 507–508.

15. Kwong-loi Shun, *Mencius and Early Chinese Thought,* p. 37.

16. See ibid.

17. This passage is not found in the extant text of *Mencius*. Knoblock maintains that we can infer this claim from Mencius's arguments with Gaozi. See Knoblock, *Xunzi,* vol. III (Stanford: Stanford University Press, 1994), p. 346, n. 16.

18. Concerning this aspect of *xing* in the *Mencius,* see Roger Ames's "The Mencian Conception of *Ren xing* 人性" pp. 143–179.

19. I will show later that Xunzi did not completely sever a tie between human morality and *tian*. Through the sense of appropriateness (*yi* 義), he seems to have restored the connection between the two. However, it should be noted here that in Xunzi's moral psychology the sense of appropriateness does not belong to the emotional aspect of *xing,* rather to the cognitive, voluntary aspect of *xin*. See chap. 4.3.

20. Here *xin* is not distinguished from other sensory organs. Later I discuss this aspect of *xin* in detail, but, for now it suffices to say that it is used in a nontechnical, ordinary sense and also can be seen as one of the dispositional aspects of *xin* given by *tian*.

Chapter 4. The Notion of *Xin*

1. Schwartz, *The World of Thought in Ancient China,* p. 184. See also Zhang Liwen, *Zhongguo zhexue fanchou fazhanshi: Tiandaopian* (Beijing: Zhongguo renmin daxue chubanshe, 1988), p. 578.

2. See *Shuowenjiezizhu* 說文解字注 (Shanghai: Shanghai guji chubanshe, 1988), p. 501.

3. Michael Loewe, ed., *Early Chinese Texts: A Biographical Guide* (Berkeley: The Society for the Study of Early China, 1993), p. 415.

4. See James Legge trans., *The She King* 詩經 (Hong Kong: Hong Kong University Press, 1982), pp. 41, 211, 259, 415.

5. Ibid., p. 342.

6. Schwartz, *The World of Thought in Ancient China,* p. 185.

7. Ibid.

8. I slightly modify Schwartz' translation; see ibid. See also Roger T. Ames and Henry Rosemont, Jr., *The Analects of Confucius: A Philosophical Translation* (New York: The Ballantine Publishing Group, Ballantine Books, 1998), 6.7, p. 105.

9. Ames and Rosemont, Jr., *Analects,* 17.22, p. 210.

10. *Mozijiaozhu* 墨子校注 上 (Beijing: Zhonghua shuju, 1993), bk. 3, chap. 2, pp. 120–121 (hereafter cited as *Mozi I*).

11. See Zhang Liwen, *Zhongguo zhexue fanchou fazhanshi,* pp. 584–585.

12. It is Confucius's real name. Kong is his family name and Qiu is his first name.

13. *Mozi I,* bk. 9, chap. 4, p. 440.

14. See Graham, *Disputers of the Tao,* pp. 261–267.

15. Loewe ed., *Early Chinese Texts,* p. 244.

16. See ibid.

17. See Shun, *Mencius and Early Chinese Thought,* p.121.

18. See Zhang Dainian 張岱年, *Zhongguo zhexue dagang* 中國哲學大綱 (Beijing: Chinese Academy of Social Sciences Press, 1982), p. 234.

19. Allyn Rickett, *Guanzi,* vol. 2 (Princeton: Princeton University Press, 1998), chap. 49, p. 46.

20. Rickett, *Guanzi,* vol. 2, chap. 49, p. 40.

21. Rickett, *Guanzi,* vol. 2, chap. 49, p. 47.

22. Hereafter, I will employ "Guanzi" to refer to the unnamed author or authors of the "Inner Workings" and the "Art of the Mind (*xinshu* 心術)" chapters.

23. Rickett construes this enigmatic passage as follows: "Within the thinking mind there is a deeper mind that can control the thinking mind and thought process" (*Guanzi,* vol. 2, p. 47, n. 113).

24. Although his expression is a little exaggerated, it seems worth hearing Schwartz' observation: "The spontaneous tendency toward goodness is embedded in an unreflective, almost Taoist-level [Daoist-level] of the heart. Yet when we speak of thought and of will (*chih* [*zhi* 志]) we are dealing with the distinctly un-Taoist [un-Daoist] *yu-wei* [*youwei* 有為] realm of deliberate goal-oriented judgment and conscious decision" (*The World of Thought,* p. 273).

25. In *A Concordance to Hsün Tzu,* we can find about 160 occurrences of the term and in all except about 30 of these, the term is easily rendered as "mind" or "heart" in the customary sense. See *A Concordance to Hsün Tzu,* pp. 113–114.

26. A. C. Cua calls this position of Xunzi's "linguistic conservatism." See A. C. Cua, *Ethical Argumentation,* p. 19.

27. My solution seems close to David Nivison's earlier position in the "Xunzi on 'Human Nature,'" and the "Critique of David B. Wong, 'Xunzi on Moral Motivation,' " in which Nivison maintains that *yi* should be construed as a bare nonmoral capacity that "enables men to form societies with hierarchical social distinctions and to apprehend an obligation as a moral obligation." Nivison, "Critique of David B. Wong, 'Xunzi on Moral Cultivation,'" in *Chinese Language, Thought, and Culture: Nivison and His Critics,* Philip J. Ivanhoe, ed. (Chicago: Open Court, 1996), p. 324. On responding to James Behuniak's criticism, Nivison retreats on this position; he, instead, claims that *yi* in this ladder passage "is not a primordial 'sense' that humans have," rather "an institutional feature exhibited by humans as a species." Nivison, "Response to James Behuniak," *Philosophy East & West,* vol. 50, no. 1, January 2000, 114. Holding that "having *yi*" does not have to be read as "having innately," Eric Hutton is largely in agreement with Nivison's later position. Eric Hutton, "Does Xunzi Have a Consistent Theory of Human Nature?," in *Virtue, Nature, and Moral Agency in the Xunzi,* p. 224. The most noteworthy in this controversy is that scholars generally assume that the whole controversial point rests on the issue of whether the ladder passage should be read as mentioning the origin of morality in terms of the concept of *yi* or not. This approach misses a larger picture of psychological structure Xunzi draws; as we have seen, Xunzi's picture of psychological structure hinges on a clear distinction between *xing* and *xin,* by which to show what is given to humans and what should be achieved. The ladder passage clearly tells that humans have a capacity to form a society, which is why humans are superior to other species. Without committing himself to a view that every necessary feature for building a harmonious society is innately given to humans, Xunzi only suggests that we have a "bare capacity to form a harmonious society," as Nivison has suggested. Because this bare capacity does not have any "positive content" or direction, it needs to be filled and guided in forming a harmonious society. At this point, I diverge from Nivison's earlier position. The reason *yi* can be an ethical disposition is because it belongs to *xin.* That's why Xunzi is able to characterize *yi* as an innate quality that makes humans superior to other species without contradicting his assertion that human *xing* is bad.

28. See Lau, *Mencius,* bk. 2, part A, chap. 6, p. 82.

29. According to Knoblock, "*shen* refers to the animating spirit within the body and to the refinement of this into intelligence and reason" (*Xunzi,* vol. 3, p. 297, n. 20).

30. John Christman ed., *The Inner Citadel: Essays on Individual Autonomy* (Oxford: Oxford University Press, 1989), p. 6.

31. *Routledge Encyclopedia of Philosophy,* vol. 1 (London: Routledge, 1998), p. 589.

32. I modify Ames's and Rosemont's translation. See Ames and Rosemont, *The Analects of Confucius,* 2.4, p. 76.

33. See Cua, *Ethical Argumentation,* pp. 139, 199–200, n. 3, 4.

34. This refers to the faculties of sense organs discussed in the chapter "Discourse on *Tian.*" See Li Disheng, *Xunzijishi,* p. 508.

35. Knoblock puts it this way: "The process of thinking, which entails selecting among the feelings that Heaven/Nature [*tian*] has given us, is crucial to overcoming

original, inborn nature [natural tendencies, *xing*]. For, as Yang Liang explains, when the mind [*xin*] has selected something, being lord over the body, it can stir the body and cause it to act in a way determined not by the inclinations of original nature [*xing*], but by the process of selection that thought naturally entails." Knoblock, *Xunzi*, vol. 3, p. 121.

36. Knoblock, *Xunzi*, vol. 3, p. 122. As mentioned earlier, Zhuangzi employs the term "*wei* 僞" in a negative sense that denotes all arbitrary, thus "false," morality and customs as opposed to natural, spontaneous *dao*. Thus, it is evident that Xunzi deliberately uses this term to criticize both Zhuangzian naturalism and the Mencian claim that the natural human propensity (*xing*) is for good.

37. We can also infer this from his assertion that "the faculty of knowing (*yizhi* 以知) is contained in human *xing*" (83/22/5, Knoblock 21.9). In light of the notion of human *xing*, *zhi* in this statement can be seen as identical with awareness (*zhi* 知).

38. See Cua, *Ethical Argumentation*, pp. 31–32.

39. I adopt Cua's rendering of *zhengzi*. See ibid.

40. As mentioned earlier, Xunzi's indebtedness to various aspects of the Mohist school is well known; his epistemological concepts and devices, such as the notion of "the type of things or categories (*lei*)" and the distinction between "awareness (*zhi* 知)" and "knowledge (*zhi* 智)" is clearly borrowed from the Mohist *Cannons*. Concerning Xunzi's indebtedness to the Mohist school, see A. C. Graham, *Later Mohist Logic, Ethics and Science* (Hong Kong: The Chinese University Press, 1978), pp. 77, 169, and Knoblock, *Xunzi*, vol. 3, p. 123.

41. Lau, *Mencius*, bk. 7, part A, chap. 15, p. 184.

42. Zhu Xi (1130–1200) is the great synthesizer of the neo-Confucian movement, specifically that of "*Lixue* (Coherence Learning)," and Wang Yangming (1472–1529) is the most prominent representative of the school of "*Xinxue* (*Xin* Learning)." See Wing Tsit-Chan, *A Source Book in Chinese Philosophy*, pp. 80, 655–656.

43. This phrase is originally from the *Great Learning*. See ibid., pp. 86, 89.

44. Cua, *Ethical Argumentation*, p. 30.

45. I adopt Van Norden's translation of the phrase "*qiuzhecongsuoke* 求者從所可." Bryan W. Van Norden, "Mengzi and Xunzi: Two Views of Human Agency," p. 174.

46. This position is held by Daoist thinkers. Knoblock finds an apt example in the *Dao De Jing*, 37: "If I cease to desire (*wuyu* 無欲) and remain still, the world will be at peace of its own accord." See Knoblock, *Xunzi*, vol. 3, p. 343, n. 92. Also see D. C. Lau, *Tao Te Ching* (Hong Kong: The Chinese University Press, 1963), chap. 37, p. 54.

47. This is the theory of Song Xing, who is regarded as a contemporary of Mencius. See Knoblock, *Xunzi*, vol. 3, p. 343, n. 93. Concerning Song Xing's philosophy in general, see Graham, *Disputers of Tao*, pp. 95–100, and Knoblock, *Xunzi*, vol. 1, pp. 59–60.

48. The following comparison between Mencius and Xunzi is indebted to Van Norden's article, "Mengzi and Xunzi: Two Views of Human Agency," pp. 161–184. Particularly see ibid., pp. 166–167, 174.

49. Lau, *Mencius,* bk. 6, part A, chap. 10, p. 166.

50. Ibid.

51. It seems evident that *zhi* 知 here refers not to awareness at the level of the sense organs but to reflective thinking at the higher level of *xin*. Li Disheng also construes *zhi* 知 as *zhi* 智. See Li Disheng, *Xunzijishi,* p. 530.

52. I adopt A. C. Cua's translation of *dali.*

53. See Knoblock, *Xunzi,* vol. 3, pp. 88–89.

54. See Ames and Rosemont, Jr., *The Analects of Confucius,* 17.8, p. 205.

55. See 2.2, p. 18.

56. A. C. Cua analyzes the phenomenon of *bi* in the *Xunzi* as follows: "*Pi* [*Bi*] arises when the mind exclusively attends to the significance of one item without proper regard for the significance of the other." Cua, *Ethical Argumentation,* p. 143.

57. More specifically, as Cua points out, while *li* 理 denotes particular rationale of each event or thing, *dao* is a holistic perspective that interconnects among particular *li* 理. See Cua, *Ethical Argumentation,* p. 62.

58. As we will soon see, although "emptiness" may be the appropriate rendition of *xu* 虛 in Zhuangzi, for Xunzi, "flexibility" or "indeterminacy" are better translations of *xu.* However, in order to avoid confusion, we will keep using the term *emptiness* as the translation of *xu.*

59. See pp. 19–22.

60. According to Yearley, "Hsün Tzu [Xunzi] accepts Chuang Tzu's [Zhuangzi's] idea that a crucial human problem is what might be called attachment," and so Xunzi modifies the notions of emptiness, unity, and placidity as the capacities of *xin* that allow it to be "subtle enough to act and yet not to be attached" as an alternative to Zhuangzi's "idea that withdrawal from the world is the only possible way to achieve detachment." Yearley, "Hsün Tzu on Mind," p. 468. For a criticism of Yearley's article, specifically his reading of Zhuangzi and the distinction between esoteric writings and exoteric writing in the *Xunzi,* see David Nivison, "Hsün Tzu and Chuang Tzu," *Chinese Texts and Philosophical Contexts,* pp. 129–142.

61. As we can see it in the following passage in which Xunzi portrays "beclouded (*bi*)" persons—that is, persons who do not keep their *xin* empty, unitary, and placid—as those whose mistakes are easily rectifiable, Xunzi does not consider the gap between ordinary *xin* and achieved *xin* to be as great as Zhuangzi does: "Someone walking along a road in the dark may see a fallen stone and think it a tiger crouching in ambush, or he may see an upright tree and think it a standing man. The darkness has beclouded the clarity of his vision. A drunk may jump across a ditch a hundred paces wide, thinking it a drain half a pace wide, or may stoop down to go out the city gate, thinking it a small doorway. The drink has disordered his spirit. Pressing against the eye while

looking at an object will make it appear double; covering the ears when listening will make silence seem like a clamor. The force applied to the sense organs has disordered them. Hence, looking down at oxen from the top of a mountain will make them appear the size of a sheep, but someone looking for sheep will not go down to lead them away. The distance has obscured their true size" (81/21/68–71, Knoblock 21.8).

62. In another explication of the notion of the placidity of *xin,* Xunzi draws an analogy between water and *xin:* "Hence, *xin* may be compared to a pan of water. If you place the pan upright and do not stir water up, the mud will sink to the bottom, and the water on top will be clear and pure enough to see your beard and eyebrows and to examine the lines on your face. But if a slight wind passes over its surface, the submerged mud will be stirred up from the bottom, and the clarity and purity of the water at the top will be disturbed so that it is impossible to obtain the correct impression of even the general outline of the face" (81/21/54–56, Knoblock 21.7b).

63. Watson, *Chuang Tzu,* chap. 13, p. 142.

64. David Nivison, "Hsun Tzu and Chuang Tzu," p. 136.

65. See Yearley, "Hsun Tzu on the Mind," pp. 468–473.

66. Cua, *Ethical Argumentation,* p.10.

Chapter 5. *Li* and Morality

1. In chapter 19 of the *Zhuangzi,* there is an anecdote about Confucius's futile attempt to rescue a man who can swim like a fish: "Confucius asked, 'At first I thought you were a ghost, but now I see you're a man. May I ask if you have some special way of staying afloat in the water?' I have no way. I began with what I was used to, grew up in what is natural to me (*xing* 性), matured in what is destined to me (*ming* 命). I go under with the swirls and come out with the eddies, following along the way the water goes and never thinking about myself. That's how I can stay afloat.' Confucius said, 'What do you mean by saying that you began with what you were used to, grew up in what is natural to me, matured in what is destined to me?' 'Having been born on dry land I am at home on dry land—it's what I am used to. Having grown up in water I am at home in water—it's natural to me. It is so without me knowing why it is so—it's destined for me.'" Watson, *Chuang Tzu,* chap. 19, pp. 204–205. Graham, *Chuang Tzu,* p. 136.

2. *Zhengming* has usually been rendered as "rectifying names" or "rectification of names." We avoid using these renditions for two reasons: first, as long as "rectification of names" implies that there is a single, correct, corresponding relation between a name and its object that allows us to "rectify" a certain name, a "prescriptive" aspect in the theory of *zhengming* is seriously undermined. Second, the topics discussed in this chapter go beyond the scope of the traditional *zhengming* theory. Xunzi deals not only with various aspects of "naming things" in themselves, but also in relation to the epistemological structure in this chapter. Thus, we render the title of chapter 21, *zhengming,* as "On the Proper Use of Names," rather than "Rectification of Names."

3. As will be shown in the subsequent citation from Knoblock, while the Ancient Kings generally refer to the founding kings of the earliest dynasties represented by Yao and Shun, the Later Kings, though sometimes including the Kings of the Three Dynasties, usually refer to the Zhou kings. See Knoblock, *Xunzi,* vol. 2, pp. 28–31.

4. Raymond Geuss offers a fine analysis of the ideas implicit in the notions of genealogy and pedigree: "A family that could trace its patent of nobility back to the 15th century might think that this pedigree showed it to be more noble than a family whose patent went back only to the 19th century." Raymond Geuss, *Morality, Culture, and History: Essays on German Philosophy* (Cambridge: Cambridge University Press, 1999), p. 3.

5. Knoblock, *Xunzi II,* pp. 28–29. We have to note that, in other chapters, Xunzi also uses "the Ancient Kings (*xianwang* 先王)" as the ultimate source of moral and institutional authority. Knoblock interprets this to be an attitude taken by Xunzi in his earlier works. See ibid., and Knoblock, "Chronology of Xunzi's Works," *Early China* 8, 1982–1983, 45.

6. Hansen divides Confucian conventionalism into two versions: one is "realist" and the other is "idealist." According to him, Confucius and Xunzi both belong to the "realist" version, and Mencius is representative of the "idealist" version. See Chad Hansen, *Language and Logic in Ancient China* (Ann Arbor: The University of Michigan Press, 1983), pp. 79–80.

7. John Makeham defines *"zhenminglun"* in terms of "nominal prescriptivism" or "nominalism." While there surely is a "prescriptive" aspect in *"zhengminglun"* which implies that "in naming one can thereby cause something to be brought about," the employment of "nominalism" seems to incite an unnecessary association with the Western metaphysical issue of whether the real entity is a particular individual or universals. For this reason, we employ "conventionalism," which does not seem to carry too many unwarranted philosophical implications. John Makeham, *Names and Actuality in Early Chinese Thought* (Albany: State University of New York Press, 1994), pp. 46–47. Concerning another argument about the inappropriateness of "nominalism" in applying to Chinese philosophy, see Hansen, *Language and Logic in Ancient China,* pp. 81–82.

8. See Hansen, *Language and Logic in Ancient China,* pp. 79–80.

9. Hall and Ames, *Thinking Through Confucius,* pp. 272–273.

10. Hansen, *Language Logic in Ancient China,* p. 80.

11. The meaning of *"bufu"* is usually understood as "not violating." There are two ways to interpret *"bufu"* in the above passage. One is to give no significant implications to *"bufu"* so that the passage is read as saying "names that are straightforward, easy, and not self-contradictory are good." Wang Xianqian and Li Disheng adopt this reading. Wang, *Xunzijijie,* xia, p. 420; Li, *Xunzijishi,* p. 518. The other is to read it as we do, that is, interpreting *"bufu"* as not violating the relationship between names and the things referred by those names. Watson and Knoblock choose this position. Watson, *Hsün Tzu,* p. 144. The reason I adopt the latter, interpretive position hinges on Xunzi's

discussion that immediately follows the above passage. Discussing various forms of things, Xunzi claims that "the examination of objects and the determination of their numbers are crucial considerations in instituting names" (84/29, Knoblock 22.2h). This shows that Xunzi not only insists on the conventionality of names but also gives a considerable weight to the relationship between names and their referents. Thus, it seems more reasonable to understand *"bufu"* as referring to the relationship between names and their referents.

12. Nivison, "Hsun Tzu and Chuang Tzu," p. 129.

13. Alvin P. Cohen, ed., "The Semasiology of Some Primary Confucian Concepts," *Selected Works of Peter A. Boodberg* (Berkeley: University of California Press, 1979), p. 34. Knoblock's explanation of the notion of *li* in Xunzi is also worth mentioning: "The term *li* 禮, usually translated ritual principles, encompasses in Xunzi's thought the highest sense of morality, duty, and social order as well as the most minor rules of good manners, the minutiae of polite forms, and insignificant, it seems to us, details of costume and dress." Knoblock, *Xunzi III,* p. 47.

14. A. S. Cua, "Dimension of *li* (propriety): reflections on an aspect of Hsün Tzu's ethics," *Philosophy East and West* 29, no. 4, Oct. 1979, 373.

15. Concerning the similarity in terms of the "perfomative" aspect between the theory of *zhengming* and the notion of *li* in Confucius, see Hall and Ames, *Thinking Through Confucius*, pp. 273–274.

16. Robert F. Campany emphasizes that "the rites' opacity" had caused Xunzi to proffer a theory about them, and nicely recapitulates various schools' positions regarding *li*. See Robert F. Campany, "Xunzi and Durkheim," in *Discourse and Practice*, ed. Frank Reynolds and David Tracy (Albany: State University of New York Press, 1992), pp. 200–202.

17. In the chapter, "Contra Physiognomy (*feishang*)," Xunzi states, "Of the instruments for distinguishing social classes, none is more important than *li* (*fenmodayuli* 分莫大於禮) (13/5/28, Knoblock 5.4)."

18. Henry Rosemont, Jr., "State and Society in the *Hsün Tzu:* A Philosophical Commentary," *Monumenta Serica* (Journal of Oriental Studies), vol. 29, 1970–1971, 53.

19. Lau, *Mencius*, bk. 2, part A, chap. 6, pp. 82–83. Considering that, for Mencius, the germ of humaneness (*renzhiduan* 仁之端) is the heart of compassion that cannot bear seeing a child fall into a well, it seems obvious that the heart of courtesy and modesty is also taken as one of the natural emotional tendencies.

20. See Eno, *The Confucian Creation of Heaven,* pp. 7–11.

21. Alasdair MacIntyre, *After Virtue* (Notre Dame: University of Notre Dame Press, 1984), p. 187.

22. Philip Ivanhoe dubs the equilibrium achieved through the function of *li* "happy symmetry" between human desires and natural resources. See Philip J. Ivanhoe, "A Happy Symmetry: Xunzi's Ethical Thought," pp. 309–322.

23. This natural order does not imply a "deep structure" that is reducible to a principle; as is the case with any other ancient Chinese philosopher's worldview, there is no evidence that Xunzi believes in a transcendental principle or order underlying the universe. As "the sun and moon shine brightly, the four seasons observe their natural precedence, the stars and planets move in ranks, and the river and streams flow (71/19/26–27, Knoblock 19.2c)," Xunzi's notion of natural order implies no more than a phenomenological, natural "pattern."

24. Commentators agree that, although Xunzi does not make an explicit remark, his target in this paragraph is the Legalists or the Legalist-oriented philosophers such as Tian Pian and Shen Dao. See Li Disheng, *Xunzijishi,* pp. 428–429. Knoblock, *Xunzi,* vol. 3, p. 320, n. 53.

25. Among several commentators who, implicitly or explicitly, support a "realist" reading of Xunzi, Philip Ivanhoe, Bryan W. Van Norden, and Paul Rakita Goldin employ this view most explicitly. Particularly see Ivanhoe, "Happy Symmetry," pp. 309–322, Van Norden "Mengzi and Xunzi," pp. 176–178, and Goldin, *Rituals of the Way: The Philosophy of Xunzi,* pp. 97–105.

26. Van Norden, "Mengzi and Xunzi," p. 177. The following passage more explicitly shows Van Norden's objectivist reading of Xunzi: "As attractive as a conventionalist reading might be in some ways, numerous passages in the *Xunzi* demonstrates that this philosopher is an objectivist and 'monist' about ritual, music, the Way, and at least some aspects of language use." See ibid.

27. Although Ivanhoe, Van Norden, and Goldin revise Watson's rendition or suggest their own translations, they all seem to base their translations on Watson's version. Since it seems possible, without revising Watson's translation, to come up with a reasonable explanation of these passages, we leave Watson's translation intact.

28. See Wm. De Bary and Irene Bloom, eds., *Sources of Chinese Tradition Second Edition, Volume 1: From Earliest Times to 1600* (New York: Columbia University Press, 1999), pp. 190–192.

29. H. G. Creel nicely captures the many levels of meaning of the notion of *fa:* "The character of *fa* has a whole series of meanings, which are closely related to the special nature of the Chinese idea of law as being that of a model, and as including not only what we regard as law but also many things that we would regard merely as regulations. This series might be represented as follows: model-method-technique-rule-regulation-law. There is a logical progression. A model is the pattern for the method of following it. Technique is method made more precise and formal. A rule describes an aspect of putting technique into practice. A regulation is a formalized rule. A law is a regulation established by authority, and often enforced by sanctions. This progression is not a series of steps, but rather a scale of infinite gradations, like a spectrum." H. G. Creel, *Shen Pu-Hai: A Chinese Political Philosopher of the Fourth Century B.C.* (Chicago: The University of Chicago Press, 1974), pp. 147–148.

30. I adopt Graham's translation. Graham, *Disputers of the Tao,* p. 282. See also W. K. Liao trans., *The Complete Works of Han Fei Tzu: A Classic of Chinese Political Science*, vol. II. (London: Arthur Probsthain, 1959), chap. XLIII, p. 212.

31. Chan, *A Source Book in Chinese Philosophy,* p. 251.

32. See Lao Siguang, *Zhongguozhexueshi* I. (Taibei: Shanminshuju, 1981), pp. 300–302.

33. I follow Schwartz's rendition of *gaizao* as "re-forming" rather than "transformation." While *hua* 化 implies an agent's voluntary transformation by virtue of his or her self-cultivation, *gaizao* implies almost "reinventing" one by forcible means or brainwashing. See, Schwartz, *The World of Thought in Ancient China,* p. 322.

34. W. K. Liao trans., *The Complete Works of Han Fei Tzu,* Vol. II, chap. XLVI, p. 239.

35. Lao Siguang, *Zhongguozhexueshi* I, p. 302.

36. Cua, citing Xunzi's phrase of "*yiyibianying* 以義變應," emphasizes the function of the sense of appropriateness as a criterion for judging the application of *li*: "'One must use *i* [*yi*, the sense of appropriateness] to cope with the changing circumstances of human life (3.5).' Whereas the exercise of *i* [the sense of appropriateness], in normal cases, may well be simply an instance of an application of a ritual rule (*li*), at issue is the judgment of the applicability of the rule rather than mere compliance with a formal requirement." Cua, *Ethical Argumentation,* pp. 23–24.

37. Schwartz, *The World of Thought in Ancient China,* p. 328.

38. Ibid.

39. Concerning the role of *li* in the formation of second-order emotions and desires, see Cua, "Dimension of *li* (propriety)," pp. 380–381. Harry G. Frankfurt, in his influential paper, "Freedom of the Will and the Concept of a Person," articulates the importance of second-order desires or volitions in characterizing the "free person" or the "autonomous person." Harry G. Frankfurt, "Freedom of the Will and the Concept of a Person," *The Importance of What We Care About* (Cambridge: Cambridge University Press, 1995), pp. 11–25.

Chapter 6. Naturalism and Autonomy

1. Recently, an increasing number of studies have appeared that attempt to rectify a one-sided picture of Kantian ethics. See Onora O'Neill, *Constructions of Reasons* (Cambridge: Cambridge University Press, 1989); Roger J. Sullivan, *Immanuel Kant's Moral Theory* (Cambridge: Cambridge University Press, 1989); Barbara Herman, *The Practice of Moral Judgment* (Cambridge: Harvard University Press, 1993); and Allen W. Wood, *Kant's Ethical Thought* (Cambridge: Cambridge University Press, 1999).

2. See Christine Korsgaard, "Excellence and obligation: a very concise history of western metaphysics 387 BC to 1887 AD," in *The Sources of Normativity* (Cambridge: Cambridge University Press, 1998), pp. 1–5.

3. John Cottingham, *Philosophy and the Good Life: Reason and the Passion in Greek, Cartesian and Psychoanalytic Ethics* (Cambridge: Cambridge University Press, 1998), pp. 9–10.

4. Anders Wedberg, *A History of Philosophy, vol. 2: The Modern Age to Romanticism* (New York: Oxford University Press, 1982), p. 7.

5. Simon, Blackburn, *The Oxford Dictionary of Philosophy* (Oxford: Oxford University Press, 1994), p. 225.

6. Ibid.

7. T. K. Seung, *Kant's Platonic Revolution in Moral and Political Philosophy* (Baltimore: The Johns Hopkins University Press, 1994), p. 1.

8. Korsgaard, "Excellence and obligation," p. 5.

9. Although the distinction between phenomena and noumena is different from the one between the natural realm and the human realm, given that Kant's concept of phenomena actually covers our ordinary understanding of nature and the natural dispositions in persons and that Kant secures the ground for human ethical realm in noumena, this phrasing seems permissible with due qualifications.

10. Otfried Höffe gives a succinct and lucid explanation of both concepts, a priori and synthetic: "Kant calls . . . knowledge which is independent of all impressions of the senses *a priori* ('from the earlier,' because the justification is free from all experience). . . . All non-analytic judgments are *synthetic:* thus all assertions are synthetic whose truth (presupposing the semantic rules of the language) cannot be determined . . . with the aid of the rules of logic. In analytic judgments the subject is only explicated by the predicate. Synthetic judgments, by contrast, expand our knowledge about the subject." Otfried Höffe, *Immanuel Kant* (Albany: State University of New York Press, 1994), pp. 39–41.

11. Henry E. Allison, "Kant, Immanuel (1724–1804)," in *The Oxford Companion to Philosophy,* ed. Ted Honderich (New York: Oxford University Press, 1995), p. 435.

12. Immanuel Kant, *Critique of Pure Reason,* trans. Norman Kemp Smith (New York: Macmillan, St. Martin's Press, 1965), Bxviii, p. 23.

13. Christine Korsgaard, "An introduction to the ethical, political, and religious thought of Kant," in *Creating the Kingdom of Ends* (Cambridge: Cambridge University Press, 1996), p. 11.

14. Kant, *Critique of Practical Reason,* trans. Lewis White Beck (New York: Macmillan Publishing Company, The Library of Liberal Arts, 3rd ed., 1993), 29, p. 28.

15. J. B. Schneewind, "Autonomy, obligation, and virtue: An overview of Kant's moral philosophy," in *The Cambridge Companion to Kant,* ed. Paul Guyer (Cambridge: Cambridge University Press, 1994), p. 315.

16. Ibid.

17. Kant, *Groundwork of the Metaphysics of Morals,* trans. Mary Gregor (Cambridge: Cambridge University Press, 1998), 4:432, p. 40.

18. See Korsgaard, "An Introduction to the ethical, political, religious thought of Kant," p. 23.

19. See Michael J. Sandel, *Liberalism and the Limits of Justice* (Cambridge: Cambridge University Press, 1992), pp. 7–11.

20. Ibid., p. 6.

21. Kant, *Groundwork of the Metaphysics of Morals,* 4:390, p. 3.

22. See Lawrence Blum, *Friendship, Altruism and Morality* (London: Routledge & Kegan Paul, 1980).

23. For Kantian response to this line of criticism, see Thomas E. Hill, Jr., "The Importance of Autonomy," in *Autonomy and Self-Respect* (Cambridge: Cambridge University Press, 1995), pp. 43–51.

24. "Organic naturalism" or "organism" should not be misconstrued as implying a teleological metaphysics that "defines the organic in terms of activity conditioned by specific ends." Instead, the organic here should be understood as emphasizing spontaneous, "correlative" relations between things rather than mechanistic, "causal" relations. See David L. Hall and Roger T. Ames, *Anticipating China,* p. 213.

25. Joseph Needham, *Science and Civilisation in China, Vol. 2: History of Scientific Thought* (Cambridge: Cambridge University Press, 1991), p. 582.

26. Frederick W. Mote, *Intellectual Foundations of China* (New York: Alfred A. Knopf, 1971), pp. 17–18.

27. Tu Wei-ming, "The Continuity of Being: Chinese Visions of Nature," in *Nature: In Asian Traditions of Thought,* ed., J. Baird Callicott and Roger T. Ames (Albany: State University of New York Press, 1989), p. 67.

28. Lau, *Mencius,* bk. 7, part A, 4, p. 182.

29. See Ibid., bk. 7, part A, 1, p. 182.

30. Schneewind, "Autonomy, obligation, and virtue," p. 313.

31. See 4.4.1.

32. Chung-ying Cheng, criticizing Kant's "Transcendental Models of knowledge and morality," explains the holistic *dao*-perspective in terms of an "Emergence Model": "[Following this Model], we could conceive morality as resulting from emergence of a right principle in our concrete grasp of a moral situation in light of all relevant facts of world and history." Chung-ying Chung, "A Theory of Confucian Selfhood: Self-Cultivation and Free Will in Confucian Philosophy," *Komparative Philosophie: Begegnungen zwischen östlichen und westlichen Denkwegen,* ed., Rolf Elberfeld, Johann Kreuzer, John Minford, and Günter Wohlfart (München: Wilhelm Fink Verlag, 1998), p. 53. n. 3.

Chapter 7. Xunzi in the History of Chinese Philosophy

1. For modern Chinese, Marxist scholars, Xunzi's thought represents a "materialist" philosophy within the Confucian tradition, as opposed to the Mencian, "mind-

only (*weixin*)" idealism. In this regard, even Marxist scholars' high evaluation of Xunzi stems from a strict application of the Marxist framework to the traditional Chinese philosophy, rather than from an evenhanded and context-sensitive reevaluation of Xunzi. See Ren Jiyu, *Zhongguo zhexueshi*, vol. 1 (Beijing: Renmin chubanshi, 1979), pp. 209–235.

2. See Knoblock, *Xunzi*, vol. 1, pp. 41–49.

3. Machle also notes that Yang Liang "gives no indication of any predecessors—for more than ten centuries!" Edward J. Machle, *Nature and Heaven in the Xunzi*, p. 11. In contrast, Zhao Qi's commentary on the *Mencius*, the first commentarial work that has been handed down to us, is dated around the third century.

4. See Wing-tsit Chan, *A Source Book in Chinese Philosophy*, p. 567, 597–600, 686. Besides neo-Confucian criticism of Xunzi, it should be noted that the fact that the major Legalists, Li Si and Han Fei, were Xunzi's students has long cast doubt on whether Xunzian philosophy has an affinity with authoritarian philosophy. As has been argued in chapter 5, the distance between Xunzi's philosophy and Han Fei's authoritarian philosophy is much greater than it first appears. It, thus, seems safe to say that later Confucians's lower evaluation of Xunzi might have something to do with Xunzi's master-disciple relationship with Han Fei and Li Si, not with the philosophically intrinsic connection between them.

5. Concerning the ritualistic trend in the Qing dynasty, see Kai-wing Chow, *The Rise of Confucian Ritualism in Late Imperial China: Ethics, Classics, and Lineage Discourse* (Stanford: Stanford University Press, 1994).

6. With the exception of Yang Liang, almost all the major commentarial works on the *Xunzi* had been produced during the Qing. See Knoblock, *Xunzi*, vol. 1, pp. 117–119.

7. For a summary of the process of the canonization of the Four Books, see John B. Henderson, *Scripture, Cannon, and Commentary: A Comparison of Confucian and Western Exegesis* (Princeton: Princeton University Press, 1991), pp. 50–51.

8. Li Zehou (1930–) is one of the most influential contemporary Chinese thinkers whose thought has been the subject of much discussion and debate among Chinese as well as Western scholars. See Woei Lien Chong, "Combining Marx with Kant: The Philosophical Anthropology of Li Zehou," *Philosophy East & West* 49, no. 2. April 1999, 120–149; and Woei Lien Chong, "Mankind and Nature in Chinese Thought: Li Zehou on the Traditional Roots of Maoist Voluntarism," *China Information*, vol. XI, nos. 2/3, 1996, 138–173. The following discussion is also indebted to Chong's careful summary of Li Zehou's thought.

9. Chong, "Combining Marx with Kant," p. 131.

10. Ibid.

11. Throughout her articles, Chong dubs this idea "voluntarism." However, since "voluntarism," in a common, Western philosophical sense, usually denotes the lack of external, constraining standards on the exercise of will, rather than the accomplishment of ends through effort of will, it does not seem appropriate to use the term to refer to

the idea of the immense power of the subjective moral will. Thus, instead of adopting "voluntarism," we choose "subjective volitionism"; because it has little currency in the history of Western philosophy, "subjective volitionism" seems safer to use in expressing the idea of the transformative power of the subjective moral will.

12. Li Zehou, *Zhongguo gudai sixiangshilun* (Beiing: Renmin Chubanshe, 1985), p. 113.

13. Chong, "Mankind and Nature in Chinese Thought," p. 154.

14. Chong, "Combining Marx with Kant," p. 136.

15. In Xunzi, we render *li* as "reasonableness." For neo-Confucians, *li* refers to more than what is reasonable; it refers to something that makes possible the whole world as it is. It is rendered as "coherence" since neo-Confucians believe that "the quality or characteristic of sticking together" is that by which a thing or the world is as it is. See Willard Peterson, "Another Look at Li," *The Bulletin of Sung-Yuan Studies* (1986), pp. 13–31.

16. Chan, *A Source Book of Chinese Philosophy,* p. 567. We have modified Wing-tsit Chan's translation.

17. Chong, "Combining Marx with Kant," p. 125.

18. Li Zehou's view can be seen as an uncritical approval of modernity. Postmodernism, postcolonialism, feminism, and ecology all criticize that Western modernity, which is based on the imperialistic universality of reason, precludes "others" such as women and non-Westerners from being the legitimate members of modernity, sacrifices desires and emotions for the construction of impartial, universalistic reason, and reifies nature as the object of exploitation. Seen from this context, Chinese organic naturalism might be regarded as providing an alternative to the Western modern worldview. For it allows reason and other faculties as well as humankind and nature to coexist in a non-antagonistic fashion. However, the criticism, without relying on the concept of modernity, seems still valid: that Chinese volitionism's tendency to reduce everything to one's self-cultivation is too subjective and idealistic.

Bibliography

Ames, Roger T. "The Mencian Conception of *Ren xing* 人性: Does It Mean 'Human Nature?'" *Chinese Texts and Philosophical Context: Essays Dedicated to Angus C. Graham*, ed. Henry Rosemont, Jr. La Salle: Open Court, 1991. 143–178.

Ames, Roger T. and Henry Rosemont, Jr. *The Analects of Confucius: A Philosophical Translation.* New York: Ballantine Books, 1998.

Behuniak, James. "Nivison and the 'Problem' in Xunzi's Ethics," *Philosophy East & West* 50, no. 1, 2000. 97–100.

Blackburn, Simon. *The Oxford Dictionary of Philosophy*. Oxford: Oxford University Press, 1994.

Bloom, Irene. "Mencian Argument on Human Nature (*Jen-Hsing*)," *Philosophy East & West* 44, no. 1, 1994. 19–53.

Blum, Lawrence. *Friendship, Atrusim and Morality*. London: Routledge & Kegan Paul, 1980.

Boodberg, Peter A. "The Semasiology of Some Primary Confucian Concepts," *Selected Works of Peter A. Boodberg*, ed. Alvin P. Cohen. Berkeley: University of California Press, 1979. 26–40.

Campany, Robert F. "Xunzi & Durkheim," *Discourse and Practice*, ed. Frank Reynolds and David Tracy. Albany: State University of New York, 1992. 197–232.

Chan, Wing-tsit. *A Source Book in Chinese Philosophy*. Princeton: Princeton University Press, 1973.

Cheng, Chung-ying. "A Theory of Confucian Selfhood: Self-Cultivation and Free Will in Confucian Philosophy," *Komparative Philosophie: Begegnungen zwischen östlichen und westlichen Denkwegen*, ed. Rolf Elberfeld, Johann Kreuzer, John Minford, and Günter Wohlfart. München: Wilhelm Fink Verlag, 1998. 51–86.

Chong, Woei Lien. "Combining Marx with Kant: The Philosophical Anthropology of Li Zehou," *Philosophy East & West* 49, no. 2, 1999. 120–149.

———. "Mankind and Nature in Chinese Thought: Li Zehou on the Traditional Roots of Maoist Voluntarism," *China Information*, vol. XI, nos. 2/3, 1996. 138–173.

Chow, Kai-wing. *The Rise of Confucian Ritualism in Late Imperial China: Ethics, Classics, and Lineage Discourse*. Stanford: Stanford University Press, 1994.

Christman, John, ed. *The Inner Citadel: Essays on Individual Autonomy*. Oxford: Oxford University Press, 1989.

A Concordance to Hsün Tzu 荀子引得. Harvard-Yenching Institute Sinological Index Series, Supplement no. 22. Beijing: Harvard-Yenching Institute, 1950.

Cottingham, John. *Philosophy and the Good Life: Reason and the Passion in Greek, Cartesian and Psychoanalytic Ethics*. Cambridge: Cambridge University Press, 1998.

Craig, Edward, ed. *Routledge Encyclopedia of Philosophy*, vol. 1. London: Routledge, 1998.

Creel, Herrlee G. *Shen Pu-Hai: A Chinese Political Philosopher of the Fourth Century B.C.* Chicago: The University of Chicago Press, 1974.

Cua, Antonio. "Dimension of *Li* (Propriety): Reflections on an Aspect of Hsün Tzu's Ethics," *Philosophy East & West* 29, no. 4, 1979. 373–394.

———. *Ethical Argumentation: A Study in Hsün Tzu's Moral Epistemology*. Honolulu: University of Hawaii Press, 1985.

de Barry, Wm. Theodore, and Irene Bloom, eds. *Sources of Chinese Tradition Second Edition, Volume One: From Earliest Times to 1600*. New York: Columbia University Press, 1999.

Ellison, Henry D. "Kant, Immanuel (1724–1804)," *The Oxford Companion to Philosophy*, ed. Ted Honderich. New York: Oxford University, 1995. 435–438.

Eno, Robert. *The Confucian Creation of Heaven: Philosophy and the Defense of Ritual Mastery*. Albany: State University of New York Press, 1990.

Frankfurt, Herry G. "Freedom of the Will and the Concept of a Person," *The Importance of What We Care About*. Cambridge: Cambridge University Press, 1995. 11–25.

Fung, Yu-lan. *A History of Chinese Philosophy*, vol. 1. Princeton: Princeton University Press, 1952.

Geuss, Raymond. *Morality, Culture, and History: Essays on German Philosophy*. Cambridge: Cambridge University Press, 1999.

Goldin, Paul Rakita. *Rituals of the Way: The Philosophy of Xunzi*. La Salle: Open Court, 1999.

Graham, Angus. C. "The Background of the Mencian Theory of Human Nature." In *Studies in Chinese Philosophy and Philosophical Literature*. Singapore: Institute of East Asian Philosophies, 1986. 7–66.

———. *Chuang Tzu: The Inner Chapters*. Boston: Mandala Books, 1981.

———. *Disputers of Tao: Philosophical Arguments in Ancient China*. La Salle: Open Court, 1991.

———. *Later Mohist Logic, Ethics and Science*. Hong Kong: Chinese University Press, 1978.

Hall, David L. and Roger Ames. *Anticipating China: Thinking through the Narratives of Chinese and Western Culture*. Albany: State University of New York Press, 1995.

———. *Thinking Through Confucius*. Albany: State University of New York Press, 1987.

Hansen, Chad. *Language and Logic in Ancient China*. Ann Arbor: The University of Michigan Press, 1983.

Henderson, John B. *Scripture, Cannon, and Commentary: A Comparison of Confucian and Western Exegesis*. Princeton: Princeton University Press, 1991.

Herman, Barbara. *The Practice of Moral Judgment*. Cambridge: Harvard University Press, 1993.

Hill, Jr., Thomas E. "The Importance of Autonomy," *Autonomy and Self-Respect*. Cambridge: Cambridge University Press, 1995. 43–51.

Höffe, Otfried. *Immanuel Kant*. Albany: State University of New York, 1994.

Hutton, Eric. "Does Xunzi Have a Consistent Theory of Human Nature?" *Virtue, Nature, and Moral Agency in the Xunzi*, eds. T. C. Kline III and Philip J. Ivanhoe. Indianapolis: Hackett Publishing Company, 2000. 220–236.

Im, Manyul. "Emotional Control and Virtue in the *Mencius*," *Philosophy East & West* 49, no. 1, 1999. 1–27.

Ivanhoe, Philip J. "A Happy Symmetry: Xunzi's Ethical Philosophy," *Journal of the American Academy of Religion* 59.2, 1991. 309–322.

———. "Human Nature and Moral Understanding in Xunzi," *International Philosophical Quarterly* 34.2, 1994. 167–175.

Kant, Immanuel. *Critique of Practical Reason* trans. Lewis White Beck. New York: Macmillan Publishing Company, The Library of Liberal Arts, 1993.

———. *Critique of Pure Reason* trans. Norman Kemp Smith. New York: Macmillan, St. Martin's Press, 1965.

———. *Groundwork of the Metaphysics of Morals* trans. Mary Gregor. Cambridge: Cambridge University Press, 1998.

Knoblock, John. "Chronology of Xunzi's Works," *Early China* 8, 1982–83. 28–52.

———. *Xunzi: A Translation and Study of the Complete Works*. Three volumes. Stanford: Stanford University Press, 1988–1994.

Korsgaard, Christine. "An introduction to the ethical, political, and religious thought of Kant," *Creating the Kingdom of Ends*. Cambridge: Cambridge University Press, 1996. 3–42.

———. "Excellence and obligation: a very concise history of western metaphysics 387 BC to 1887 AD," *The Source of Normativity*. Cambridge: Cambridge University Press, 1998. 1–5.

Lao, Siguang 勞思光. *Zhongguo zhexueshi* 中國哲學史, vol. 1. Taibei: Shanmin shuju, 1981.

Lau, D. C. trans. *Mencius*. New York: Penguin Books, 1970.

———. trans. *Tao Te Ching*. Hong Kong: The Chinese University Press, 1963.

Legge, Jame trans. *The She King* 詩經, *The Chinese Classics*, vol. 3. Hong Kong: Hong Kong University Press, 1982.

Li, Disheng 李滌生. *Xunzijishi* 荀子集釋. Taibei: Xuesheng Shuju, 1979.

Li, Zehou 李擇厚. *Zhongguo gudai sixiangshilun* 中國古代思想史論. Beijing: Renmin Chubanshe, 1985.

Liao, W. K. trans. *The Complete Works of Han Fei Tzu*, vol. I–II. London: Arthur Probsthain, 1959.

Loewe, Michael, ed. *Early Chinese Texts: A Bibliographical Guide*. Berkeley: The Society for the Study of Early China and The Institute of East Asian Studies, University of California, Berkeley, 1993.

Machle, Edward J. *Nature and Heaven in the Xunzi*. Albany: State University of New York Press, 1993.

MacIntyre, Alasdair. *After Virtue*. Notre Dame: University of Notre Dame Press, 1984.

Makeham, John. *Nature and Actuality in Early Chinese Thought*. Albany: State University of New York, 1994.

Mote, Frederick W. *Intellectual Foundations of China*. New York: Alfred A. Knopf, 1971.

Mozi jiaozhu shang 墨子校注上. Beijing: Zhonghua shuju, 1993.

Needham, Joseph. *Science and Civilisation in China, Vol. 2: History of Scientific Thought*. Cambridge: Cambridge University Press, 1991.

Nivison, David S. "Hsun Tzu and Chuang Tzu," *Chinese Texts and Philosophical Contexts: Essays Dedicated to Angus C. Graham*. Ed. Henry Rosemont, Jr. La Salle: Open Court, 1991. 129–142.

———. "Xunzi on 'Human Nature,'" *The Ways of Confucianism: Investigations in Chinese Philosophy*. Ed. Bryan W. Van Norden. La Salle: Open Court, 1996. 203–213.

———. "Critique of David B. Wong, 'Xunzi on Moral Motivation,'" *Chinese Language, Thought, and Culture: Nivison and His Critics*. Ed. Philip J. Ivanhoe. Chicago: Open Court, 1996. 323–331.

O'Neill, Onora. *Construction of Reasons*. Cambridge: Cambridge University Press, 1989.

Peterson, Willard. "Another Look at Li," *The Bulletin of Sung-Yuan Studies*, 1986. 13–31.

Ren, Jiyu 任繼愈. *Zhongguo zhexueshi* 中國哲學史, vol. 1. Beijing: Renmin chubanshi, 1979.

Rickett, Allyn. trans. *Guanzi*, vol. 1–2. Princeton: Princeton University Press, 1985–98.

Rosemont, Jr., Henry. "State and Society in the Hsün Tzu: A Philosophical Commentary," *Monumenta Serica* (Journal of Oriental Studies) 29, 1970–71. 38–78.

Schneewind, J. B. "Autonomy, obligation, and virtue: An overview of Kant's moral philosophy," *The Cambridge Companion to Kant*. Ed. Paul Guyer. Cambridge: Cambridge University Press, 1994. 309–341.

Schwartz, Benjamin I. *The World of Thought in Ancient China*. Cambridge: the Belknap Press of Harvard University Press, 1985.

Sandel, Michael J. *Liberalism and the Limits of Justice*. Cambridge: Cambridge University Press, 1992.

Seung, T. K. *Kant's Platonic Revolution in Moral and Political Philosophy*. Baltimore: The Johns Hopkins University Press, 1994.

Shun, Kwong-loi. *Mencius and Early Chinese Thought*. Stanford: Stanford University Press, 1997.

Shuwon jiezizhu 說文解字注. Shanghai: Shanghai guji chubanshi, 1988.

Sullivan, Roger J. *Immanuel Kant's Moral Theory*. Cambridge: Cambridge University Press, 1989.

Tu, Wei-ming. "The Continuity of Being: Chinese Visions of Nature," *Nature: In Asian Traditions of Thought*. Ed. J. Baird Callicott and Roger Ames. Albany: State University of New York Press, 1989. 67–78.

Van Norden, Bryan W. "Mengzi and Xunzi: Two Views of Human Agency," *International Philosophical Quarterly* 32, no. 2, 1992. 161–184.

Wang, Xianqian 王先謙. *Xunzi jijie, shangxia* 荀子集解, 上下. Beijing: Zhonghua shuju, 1996.

Watson, Burton. trans. *The Complete Works of Chuang Tzu*. New York: Columbia University Press, 1968.

———. trans. *Han Fei Tzu: Basic Writings*. New York: Columbia University Press, 1964.

———. trans. *Hsün Tzu: Basic Writings*. New York: Columbia University Press, 1963.

Wedberg, Anders. *A History of Philosophy, vol. 2: The Modern Age to Romanticism*. New York: Oxford University Press, 1982.

Wood, Allen W. *Kant's Ethical Thought*. Cambridge: Cambridge University Press, 1999.

Yearley, Lee. "Hsün Tzu on the Mind: His Attempted Synthesis of Confucianism and Taoism," *Journal of Asian Studies* 39, no. 3, 1980. 465–480.

Zhang, Dainian 張岱年. *Zhongguo zhexue dagang* 中國哲學大綱. Beijing: Chinese Academy of Social Sciences, 1982.

Zhang, Liwen 張立文. *Zhongguo zhexue fanchou fazhanshi: Tiandaopian* 中國哲學範疇史: 天道篇. Beijing: Zhongguo renmin daxue chubanshi, 1988.

Index

www.ingramcontent.com/pod-product-compliance
Lightning Source LLC
LaVergne TN
LVHW101627040926
847296LV00026B/122
* 9 7 8 0 7 9 1 4 6 1 9 8 3 *